Praise for *Grandma Gatewood's Walk*

"Before Cheryl Strayed, there was Grandma Gatewood. Ben Montgomery lets us walk with her—tattered sneakers, swollen ankles, and not an ounce of self-pity—and with each step experience our conflicted relationship with nature, the meanness and generosity of humanity, and the imperative to keep moving. This book makes me long for my backpacking days, and grateful for writers who keep history and spirit alive."
—Jacqui Banaszynski, Knight Chair in Editing,
Missouri School of Journalism

"Ben Montgomery adds his name to those famous Americans—from Henry David Thoreau to Rosa Parks to Fats Domino to Forrest Gump—who have celebrated the revolutionary power of walking."
—Roy Peter Clark, author of *The Glamour of Grammar:
A Guide to the Magic and Mystery of Practical English*

"Montgomery's compelling tale secures Grandma Gatewood's place in the American pantheon as a cousin of John Henry and Johnny Appleseed."
—Andrea Pitzer, author of *The Secret History of Vladimir Nabokov*

"The whole saga of Grandma Gatewood, from her years in an abusive marriage to her triumph as a hiking superstar, is a great story, beautifully told." —*Tampa Bay Times*

"Details on Emma's hike, health, and reflections on the times make this book a compelling, fast read." —*National Parks Traveler*

"A powerful tale about finding solace not only in nature, but also in the generosity of strangers—an ethic that still exists on the trail today." —*America*

T0025725

GRANDMA GATEWOOD'S WALK

The Inspiring Story of the Woman
Who Saved the Appalachian Trail

BEN MONTGOMERY

CHICAGO
REVIEW
PRESS

Published by Chicago Review Press, Incorporated
814 North Franklin Street
Chicago, Illinois 60610
ISBN 978-1-61374-718-6 (cloth)
ISBN 978-1-61373-499-5 (paper)

Library of Congress Cataloging-in-Publication Data
Montgomery, Ben.
  Grandma Gatewood's walk : the inspiring story of the woman who saved the
Appalachian Trail / Ben Montgomery.
       p. cm.
  Includes bibliographical references and index.
  ISBN 978-1-61374-718-6 (cloth)
  1. Gatewood, Emma Rowena Caldwell, -1973. 2. Hikers—Appalachian
Trail—Biography. 3. Women conservationists—Appalachian Trail—Biogra-
phy. 4. Appalachian Trail—History. I. Title.

  GV199.92.G35M66 2014
  796.51092—dc23
  [B]

                              2013037551

Cover design: Debbie Berne Design
Cover photo: Gatewood family collection, courtesy Lucy Gatewood Seeds
Interior design: PerfecType, Nashville, TN
Map design: Chris Erichsen

Printed in the United States of America

For Jennifer

the Berkshires, the Green Mountains, the White Mountains, the Mahoosuc Range. Saddleback, Bigelow, and finally—five million steps away—Katahdin.

And between here and there: a bouquet of ways to die.

Between here and there lurked wild boars, black bears, wolves, bobcats, coyotes, backwater outlaws, and lawless hillbillies. Poison oak, poison ivy, and poison sumac. Anthills and black flies and deer ticks and rabid skunks, squirrels, and raccoons. And snakes. Black snakes, water moccasins, and copperheads. And rattlers; the young man who hiked the trail four years before told the newspapers he'd killed at least fifteen.

There were a million heavenly things to see and a million spectacular ways to die.

Two people knew Emma Gatewood was here: the cabdriver and her cousin, Myrtle Trowbridge, with whom she had stayed the night before in Atlanta. She had told her children she was going on a walk. That was no lie. She just never finished her sentence, never offered her own offspring the astonishing, impossible particulars.

All eleven of them were grown, anyhow, and independent. They had their own children to raise and bills to pay and lawns to mow, the price of participation in the great, immobile American dream.

She was past all that. She'd send a postcard.

If she told them what she was attempting to do, she knew they'd ask *Why?* That's a question she'd face day and night in the coming months, as word of her hike spread like fire through the valleys, as newspaper reporters learned of her mission and intercepted her along the trail. It was a question she'd playfully brush off every time they asked. And *how* they'd ask. Groucho Marx would ask. Dave Garroway would ask. *Sports Illustrated* would ask. The Associated Press would ask. The United States Congress would ask.

Why? Because it was there, she'd say. Seemed like a good lark, she'd say.

her small garden and looked after her grandchildren, biding her time until she could get away.

When she finally could, it was 1955, and she was sixty-seven years old.

She stood five foot two and weighed 150 pounds and the only survival training she had were lessons learned earning calluses on her farm. She had a mouth full of false teeth and bunions the size of prize marbles. She had no map, no sleeping bag, no tent. She was blind without her glasses, and she was utterly unprepared if she faced the wrath of a snowstorm, not all that rare on the trail. Five years before, a freezing Thanksgiving downpour killed more than three hundred in Appalachia, and most of them had houses. Their bones were buried on these hillsides.

She had prepared for her trek the only way she knew how. The year before, she worked at a nursing home and tucked away what she could of her twenty-five-dollar-a-week paycheck until she finally earned enough quarters to draw the minimum in social security: fifty-two dollars a month. She had started walking in January while living with her son Nelson in Dayton, Ohio. She began walking around the block, and extended it a little more each time until she was satisfied by the burn she felt in her legs. By April she was hiking ten miles a day.

Before her, now, grew an amazing sweep of elms, chestnuts, hemlocks, dogwoods, spruces, firs, mountain ashes, and sugar maples. She'd see crystal-clear streams and raging rivers and vistas that would steal her breath.

Before her stood mountains, more than three hundred of them topping five thousand feet, the ancient remnants of a range that hundreds of millions of years before pierced the clouds and rivaled the Himalayas in their majesty. The Unakas, the Smokies, Cheoahs, Nantahalas. The long, sloping Blue Ridge; the Kittatinny Mountains; the Hudson Highlands. The Taconic Ridge and

They hit a steep incline, a narrow gravel road, and made it within a quarter mile of the top of the mountain before the driver killed the engine.

She collected her supplies and handed him five dollars, then one extra for his trouble. That cheered him up. And then he was gone, taillights and dust, and Emma Gatewood stood alone, an old woman on a mountain.

Her clothes were stuffed inside a pasteboard box and she lugged it up the road to the summit, a few minutes away by foot. She changed in the woods, slipping on her dungarees and tennis shoes and discarding the simple dress and slippers she'd worn during her travels. She pulled from the box a drawstring sack she'd made back home from a yard of denim, her wrinkled fingers doing the stitching, and opened it wide. She filled the sack with other items from the box: Vienna Sausage, raisins, peanuts, bouillon cubes, powdered milk. She tucked inside a tin of Band-Aids, a bottle of iodine, some bobby pins, and a jar of Vicks salve. She packed the slippers and a gingham dress that she could shake out if she ever needed to look nice. She stuffed in a warm coat, a shower curtain to keep the rain off, some drinking water, a Swiss Army knife, a flashlight, candy mints, and her pen and a little Royal Vernon Line memo book that she had bought for twenty-five cents at Murphy's back home.

She threw the pasteboard box into a chicken house nearby, cinched the sack closed, and slung it over one shoulder.

She stood, finally, her canvas Keds tied tight, on May 3, 1955, atop the southern terminus of the Appalachian Trail, the longest continuous footpath in the world, facing the peaks on the blue-black horizon that stretched toward heaven and unfurled before her for days. Facing a mean landscape of angry rivers and hateful rock she stood, a woman, mother of eleven and grandmother of twenty-three. She had not been able to get the trail out of her mind. She had thought of it constantly back home in Ohio, where she tended

1

PICK UP YOUR FEET

She packed her things in late spring, when her flowers were in full bloom, and left Gallia County, Ohio, the only place she'd ever really called home.

She caught a ride to Charleston, West Virginia, then boarded a bus to the airport, then a plane to Atlanta, then a bus from there to a little picture-postcard spot called Jasper, Georgia, "the First Mountain Town." Now here she was in Dixieland, five hundred miles from her Ohio home, listening to the rattle and ping in the back of a taxicab, finally making her ascent up the mountain called Oglethorpe, her ears popping, the cabbie grumbling about how he wasn't going to make a penny driving her all this way. She sat quiet, still, watching through the window as miles of Georgia blurred past.

CONTENTS

We do not go into the woods
to rough it; we go to smooth it.
We get it rough enough at home.
—GEORGE WASHINGTON SEARS

Now or never.
—HENRY DAVID THOREAU

I get faster as I get older.
—EMMA GATEWOOD

She'd never betray the real reason. She'd never show those news-papermen and television cameras her broken teeth or busted ribs, or talk about the town that kept dark secrets, or the night she spent in a jail cell. She'd tell them she was a widow. Yes. She'd tell them she found solace in nature, away from the grit and ash of civilization. She'd tell them that her father always told her, "Pick up your feet," and that, through rain and snow, through the valley of the shadow of death, she was following his instruction.

— — — — — —

She walked around the summit of Mount Oglethorpe, studying the horizon, the browns and blues and grays in the distance. She walked to the base of a giant, sky-reaching monument, an obelisk made from Cherokee marble.

She read the words etched on one side:

IN GRATEFUL RECOGNITION OF THE ACHIEVEMENTS OF JAMES EDWARD OGLETHORPE WHO BY COURAGE, INDUSTRY AND ENDURANCE FOUNDED THE COMMONWEALTH OF GEORGIA IN 1732

She turned her back on the phallic monument and lit off down the trail, a path that split through ferns and last year's leaves and walls of hardwoods sunk deep in the earth. She walked quite a while before she came upon the biggest chicken farm she had ever seen, row upon row of long, rectangular barns, alive with babble and bordered by houses where the laborers slept, immigrants and sons of the miners and blue-collar men and women who made their lives in these mountains.

She had walked herself to thirst, so she knocked on one of the doors. The man who answered thought she was a little loony, but he gave her a cool drink. He told her there was a store nearby, said it

5

was just up the road. She set off, but didn't see one. Night fell, and for the first time, she was alone in the dark.

The trail cut back, but she missed the identifying blaze and kept walking down a gravel road; after two miles, she came upon a farmhouse. Two elderly folks, a Mr. and Mrs. Mealer, were kind enough to let her stay for the night. She would have been forced to sleep in the forest, prone to the unexpected, had she not lost track.

She set off early the next morning, as the sun threw a blue haze on the hills, after thanking the Mealers. She knew she had missed the switchback, so she hiked back the way she had come for about two miles and all along the roadside she saw beautiful sweetshrub blooming, smelling of allspice. She caught the trail again and lugged herself back up to the ridge, where she reached a level stretch and pressed down hard on her old bones, foot over foot, going fifteen miles before dark. The pain was no problem, not yet, for a woman reared on farm work.

She stumbled upon a little cardboard shack, disassembled it, and set up several of the pieces on one end to block the angry wind. The others she splayed on the ground for a bed. As soon as she lay down, her first night in the woods, the welcoming party came calling. A tiny field mouse, the size of a golf ball, began scratching around her. She tried to scare the creature away, but it was fearless. When she finally found sleep, the mouse climbed upon her chest. She opened her eyes and there he was, standing erect on her breast, just two strange beings, eye to eye, in the woods.

━ ━ ━ ━ ━

A hundred years before Emma Gatewood stomped through, before there was even a trail, pioneers pushed west over the new country's oldest mountains, through Cherokee land, the determined Irish and

Scottish and English families driving toward the sinking sun, and some of them falling behind. Some of them settling.

They made these mountains, formed more than a billion years before of metamorphic and igneous rock, their home. Appalachia, it was called, a term derived from a tribe of Muskhogean Indians called the Appalachee, the "people on the other side."

The swath was beautiful and rugged, and those who stayed lived by ax and plow and gun. On the rich land they grew beets and tomatoes, pumpkins and squash, field peas and carrots. But mostly they grew corn. By the 1940s, due to the lack of education and rotation, the land was drained of its nutrients and crops began to fail.

But the people remained, buckled in by the mountains.

Those early settlers were buried on barren hillsides. The threadbare lives of their sons and daughters were set in grooves, a day's drive from 60 percent of the US population but cut off by topography from outside ideas. They wore handmade clothing and ate corn pone, hickory chickens, and fried pies. The pigs they slaughtered in the fall showed up on plates all winter as sausage and bacon and salted ham. They went to work in the mines and mills, risking death each day to light the homes and clothe the children of those better off while their own sons and daughters did schoolwork by candlelight and wore patches upon patches.

Mining towns, mill towns, and small industrial centers bloomed between the mountains, and the dirt roads and railroads soon stitched the little communities together. They were proud people, most of them, the durable offspring of survivors. They lived suspended between heaven and earth, and they knew the call of every bird, the name of every tree, and where the wild herbs grew in the forest. They also knew the songs in the church hymnals without looking, and the difference between predestination and free will, and the recipe for corn likker.

They resisted government intervention, and when taxes grew unjust, they struck out with rakes, rebellion, and secrecy. When President Rutherford B. Hayes tried to implement a whiskey tax in the late 1870s, a great fit of violence exploded in Appalachia between the moonshiners and the federal revenuers that lasted well through Prohibition in the 1920s. The lax post–Civil War law and order gave the local clans plenty of leeway to shed blood over a misunderstanding or a misfired bullet. Grudges held tight, like cold tree sap.

When the asphalt was laid through the bottomland, winding rivers of road, it opened the automobile-owning world to new

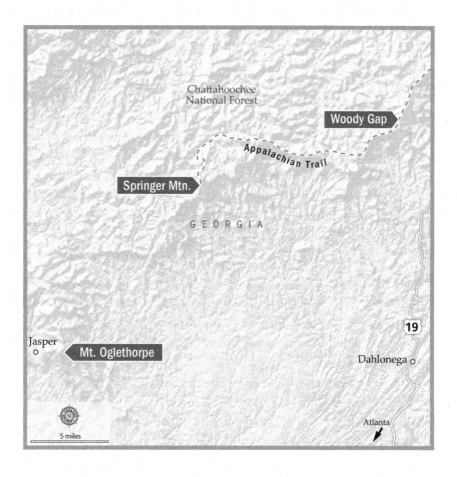

pictures of poverty and hard luck. The rest of America came to bear witness to coal miners and moonshiners, and a region in flux. Poor farming techniques and a loss of mining jobs to machines prompted an exodus from Appalachia in the 1950s. Those who stayed behind were simply rugged enough, or conniving enough, to survive.

This was Emma Gatewood's course, a footpath through a misunderstood region stitched together on love and danger, hospitality and venom. The route was someone else's interpretation of the best way to cross a lovely and rugged landscape, and she had accepted the invitation to stalk her predecessors—this civilian army of planners and environmentalists and blazers—and, in a way, to become one of them, a pilgrim herself. She came from the foothills, and while she didn't know exactly what to expect, she wasn't a complete stranger here.

— — — — — —

Her legs were sore when she set off a few minutes after 9:00 AM on May 5, trying to exit Georgia. She hiked the highlands until she could go no farther. Her feet had swollen. She found a lean-to near a freshwater spring where she washed out her soiled clothes. She filled her sack full of leaves and plopped it on a picnic table for a makeshift bed.

The next morning, she started before the sun peeked over the hills. The trail, through the heart of Cherokee country, was lined by azaleas, and when the sunbeams touched down they became flashes of supernatural pinks and purples in the gray-brown forest. Once in a while, she'd stop mid-step to watch a white-tailed buck bound gracefully across her path and disappear into the woods. Once in a while, she'd spot a copperhead coiled in the leaves and she'd catch her breath and provide the creature a wide berth.

That night she drank buttermilk and ate cornbread, the charity of a man in town, and spent the night at the Doublehead Gap Church, in the house of the Lord. That's how it was some places. They'd open their iceboxes and church doors and make you feel at home. Some places, but not all.

She was off again the next day, past a military base where soldiers had built dugouts and stretched barbed wire all over the mountains, a surreal juxtaposition of nature and the brutality of man. She pressed on through Woody Gap, approaching the state line. She was joined there by an old, tired-looking mutt, and she didn't mind the company.

She climbed a mountain, cresting after 7:00 PM, the sun falling. She'd have to find a place to stay soon. She followed the bank of a creek down into the valley, where several small houses stood. They were ugly little things, but there was a chance one would yield a bed, or at least a few bales of hay. Anything was better than shaking field mice out of her hair in the morning.

In the yard of one of the puny homes, she noticed a woman chopping wood. It looked as if the woman's hair had not been combed in weeks, and her apron was so dirty it could have stood on its own. Her face was covered with grime and she was chewing tobacco, spitting occasionally in the dirt.

The woman stopped as Emma approached.

Have you room for a guest tonight? Emma asked.

We've never turned anyone away, the woman said.

Emma followed her onto the porch, where an old man sat in the shade. He wasn't nearly as dirty as the woman, and he looked intelligent—and suspicious. This was the tricky, treacherous part of the trail, scouting for a bed among strangers. She had not prepared for this part of the experience, for she never knew these negotiations would be necessary. There, on the strangers' porch, she wasn't afraid so much as embarrassed. She told the man her name.

You have credentials? the man asked.

She fetched her social security card from her sack and handed it over. He studied the card as the mutt that followed her down the hollow sniffed out a comfortable spot on the porch. Emma fished out some pictures of her family, her children and grandchildren, and presented those, too, for further proof that she was who she said she was. But the man was suspicious.

Is Washington paying you to make this trip? the man asked.

No, Emma said.

She told him she was doing it for herself, and she had every intention of hiking all 2,050 miles of it, to the end. She just needed a place to spend the night.

Does your family approve of what you're doing? asked he.

They don't know, said she.

He regarded her, an old woman in tapered dungarees and a button-up shirt, her long, gray hair a mess. Her thin lips and fat, fleshy earlobes. Her brow protruding enough to shade her eyes at their corners. She hadn't seen a mirror in days, but she reckoned she looked hideous.

You'd better go home, then, he said. *You can't stay here.*

There wasn't any use in fighting. She knew where she was. She hefted her sack onto her shoulder again, turned her back on the man and his worn-out wife, and started walking.

2

GO HOME, GRANDMA

The Cherokees were gone, most of them relocated at gunpoint to Oklahoma, but their stories still whipped through the passes of the ancient Blue Ridge Mountains of North Georgia.

In the beginning, as the native creation story had it, the earth hung from the heavens by four cords and the surface of the earth was covered by water until a beetle dived down and brought up mud, creating land, which spread in every direction. One by one, emissaries visited from the sky realm to see if the earth was inhabitable, until a great vulture made an exploratory trip. When he tired, he flew so low his wings brushed the earth, punching valleys on the down thrust and bringing forth mountains, these mountains, on the updraft.

When the land finally dried and plants and animals came they were given instructions to stay awake for seven nights, to keep

13

watch over their new habitat. Nearly all were awake the first night, but several had fallen asleep by the next, and more by the third, and then others. By the seventh night, only the pine, spruce, laurel, holly, and cedar plants had stayed awake to the end, and they were rewarded medicinal properties and evergreen foliage; the rest were punished and made to lose their "hair" each winter. Of the animals, only the panther, owl, and a few others remained alert; they received the power to see in the dark, to own the night.

Darkness was falling. Emma walked as fast as she could, feeling alone, and the trail carried her over the mountain until she finally found a narrow logging road and hurried down it, keeping in the middle, until she came upon some large machinery and a shed about 10:30 PM. She crept inside, spread her blanket on the floor, and secured the door. She heard dogs barking, then a pickup truck, but she stayed still. In the morning, when she finally woke, she stepped outside. In the soft light of dawn, she could see that she'd found her way into the middle of a summer camp, but it appeared to be vacant, no camp counselors blowing whistles and no children doing morning exercises.

Her own children had no idea she was here. She wasn't even sure if all eleven of them knew about the Appalachian Trail, or how the footpath had been calling her, how she'd been captivated by the fact that no woman had yet hiked it alone.

They knew she loved to walk, that she'd stalk through the hills of Gallia County, awed by the stillness and quiet of the forests. They remembered stomping through the woods with her when they were young, when she'd urge them to listen for birdsongs and teach them to watch for snakes around blackberry bushes and point out the medicinal properties of wild plants, as if she were preparing them for their own journeys.

Her resolve, hardened by years of white-knuckle work, was intact. She trod along, through the ferns and galax, ground cedar and May apple, through great patches of oak and hickory and poplar trees. The flowers were popping: the bloodroot, trillium, violets, bluets, lady's slipper, and beardtongue. As she approached the edge of the forest she saw something that beckoned her on, something she wouldn't see again for another two thousand miles, like a gift from the Cherokee: a pink dogwood.

She had told no one of her plans for the long walk that year, for fear they'd worry or try to stop her. She hadn't even told them about the year before, about her failure. That would be her secret, too, a pact between her and God and the park rangers in the Maine wilderness who saved her life.

— — — — — —

She first laid eyes on the trail in a doctor's office back home, inside a discarded *National Geographic* from August 1949, and the nineteen-page spread with color photographs was a window to another place. The photos showed a bear cub clinging to a tree by a trail blaze, shirtless men scrambling up lichen-speckled boulders above the tree line in Maine, teenaged hikers atop rocks at Sherburne Pass in Vermont, hikers on an overlook at Grandeur Peak, a "girl hiker" inching through a crevice near Bear Mountain in New York. She read that a hiker in the Great Smoky Mountains had looked down into a deep canyon and had seen a lank man hoeing a corn patch. The steep cliffs made the hollow seem inaccessible, so the hiker shouted, "How'd you get down there?" "Don't know," came the reply. "I was born yere."

She read that the "soul-cheering, foot-tempting trail" was as wide as a Mack truck, that food was easy to come by, and that trailside shelters were plentiful and spaced within a day's walk from one another.

"The Appalachian Trail, popularly the 'A.T.,' is a public pathway that rates as one of the seven wonders of the outdoorsman's world," the article gushed. "Over it you may 'hay foot, straw foot' from

Mount Katahdin, with Canada on the horizon, to Mount Ogle-thorpe, which commands the distant lights of Atlanta."

The old woman had been captivated.

"Planned for the enjoyment of anyone in normal good health," it read, "the A.T. doesn't demand special skill or training to traverse."

By the time the article was published in 1949, just one man, a twenty-nine-year-old soldier named Earl V. Shaffer, had officially reported hiking the trail's entire length in a single, continuous journey. In the seven years since Shaffer's celebrated hike, only five others had achieved the same. All were men.

Emma intended to change that.

"I thought that although I was sixty-six," she would write later in her diary, "I would try it."

She didn't tell anyone what she planned to do and she gathered what she thought she could not do without, not what one was supposed to take on a two-thousand-mile hike. Those who had come before arrived with mail-order rucksacks and sleeping bags and tents and mess kits. Not Emma. Her little sack weighed seventeen pounds.

Since it was July 1954 by the time she was ready to set out on the five-month journey, she decided to start in the north and race the cold south. She caught the 6:15 AM Greyhound out of Gallia County for Pittsburgh, and there caught the New York Express to Manhattan, then another bus to Augusta, Maine, arriving early the following morning. She caught another bus from Augusta to Bangor and checked into the Hotel Penobscot for the night and gave the man behind the counter $4.50.

The next morning, July 10, she caught a cab to Pitman camp and arrived about 10:30 AM, then climbed Mount Katahdin, the northern terminus of the trail. Three and a half hours later she was back down, just before dark. A young couple invited her to share broiled hot dogs and pea beans baked with molasses and salt pork. Then she spread her blanket and drifted off to sleep under a lean-to at Katahdin Stream Campground, where the creek sings all night.

The next morning, before the sun peeked into the valley, she left her suitcase with a park ranger, gave him a dollar, and asked him to send it back to Ohio. Then she set off for York Camp, a sporting cabin on the west branch of the Penobscot River. A few miles in, she realized she had packed too many clothes so she emptied her bag, stuffed her extras into a box, and asked the folks at York Camp to mail them back to Ohio.

She hiked from there to Rainbow Lake, some thirteen miles farther, and a nice family at the campgrounds treated the bedraggled old woman to roast beef and pie. She decided to take the next day off and stayed two nights.

The next morning she started early. When she came to a weather-rotted sign, she took the wrong trail. She didn't know that the Appalachian Trail was marked with white blazes and wound up walking far off course. Just before noon, she popped out of the forest and into a patch of bracken and realized she had lost her way. She searched for an hour and a half in the wilderness but couldn't find the path. She climbed a knoll in an open space and built a fire and lay on the ground. She whistled and sang a little and nibbled on the raisins and peanuts she'd brought along.

"I did not worry if it was to be the end of me," she wrote in her diary. "It was as good a place as any."

After lunch, she went in search of water and disappeared deeper into the wilderness, following game trails through thick summer vegetation. As night fell, she found a rock and lay down to try to rest. When bands of rain blew through, she stood until they passed.

She tried more paths the next morning, exerting precious energy on a second wasted day, none leading her to the trail she had taken in, her food supply running short. She uprooted bracken to make a bed under an overturned rowboat she found leaning against some evergreen trees. She lit a fire, filled a coffee can with water, and doused the flames, hoping the smoke signals would alert other hikers or the rangers at Baxter State Park, but no one came.

She decided to take a bath in a small pond and she placed her eyeglasses on a rock. She forgot where she'd put them, and took a bad step, crushing a lens. She tried to patch it with a Band-Aid, but she could barely see.

She kept the fire going a few more hours, until eleven o'clock, but the wood was running short and she was growing tired. She ate the last of her food and lay down to rest, covering her face to keep the black flies away. Then she heard it.

An airplane came into view, flying low above the trees, the thump of its propeller echoing off the mountains. She jumped to her feet and waved a white cloth to try to flag the plane. And then it was gone.

She lay back down and closed her eyes. She was out of food, and almost out of hope, lost in a vast wilderness not even thirty miles from where she had begun. What would she say when she got back home, if she made it back home? What would she tell people?

She didn't know it, but the ranger at Rainbow Lake had radioed the next camp, eight miles away, asking for an update when Emma arrived. When she didn't come, the foresters launched a search.

Emma looked around for wood sorrel, which could be eaten for nourishment, but couldn't find any. Nor could she find early chokeberries, blueberries, or cranberries, which had yet to bloom. She decided to try to find the trail one more time. She collected her things and started back the way she had come. By luck or miracle, she found the path back toward the camp and set off. She hiked for hours and finally arrived at Rainbow Lake by 7:00 PM, where she found a group of men throwing horseshoes.

Four Baxter State Park rangers had been frantically searching for her. They'd come across her camp while she was out scouting and they found traces of her fire. They had combed the woods, calling out for her, but she never heard them.

Welcome to Rainbow Lake, one of the men said. *You've been lost.*

Not lost, Emma said. *Just misplaced.*

The rangers, all men, were annoyed. They started telling her she should go home.

I wouldn't want my mother doing this, one of them said.

She had broken glasses, no food, and not much money. Maybe they were right. Maybe she should quit.

Two of the rangers helped her into their monoplane and flew her to a nearby lake where the Baxter Park superintendent was waiting. He took her to the railroad station in Millinocket and put her on a train back to Bangor where she staggered through the streets, people casting sideways glances her way, and into the Penobscot Hotel, the same place she'd stayed seven long days before.

The man behind the counter said the hotel was full.

Have you tried any other place? he asked.

No, she said. *I stayed here last week.*

The man scratched around in some papers on the counter.

They won't want that room tonight, he said. *You can have it.*

A bellboy escorted Emma upstairs.

Don't you remember me? she asked him.

Yes, he said.

I've been climbing mountains, she said.

She closed her door and dropped her bag and walked to the mirror. She barely recognized the woman staring back at her. Broken glasses. A black fly had bit her near the eye and it was bruised. Her sweater was full of holes. Her hair was a mess. Her feet were swollen. She thought she looked like a drunk out of the gutter. A vagabond. A sixty-six-year-old failure.

She'd tell no one about this.

— — — — — —

This time would be different. She had learned hard lessons.

She had been on the trail eight days when she caught a ride, from a man and woman named Jarrett who were picking up fertilizer near where a truck had spilled its load. They allowed her to stay the night at their home and drove her back to the trail the next morning, to the same spot from which she'd left, and sent her packing with a mess of corn pone. She walked twenty miles that day, finally reaching Hightower Gap as a spring thunderstorm moved

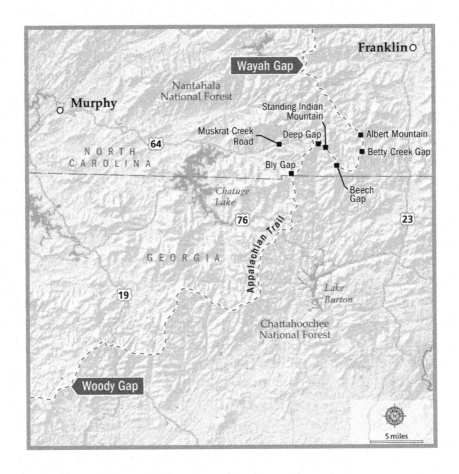

in. She made her bed on some boards under a cement picnic table, but she rolled back and forth all night, trying helplessly to stay out of the rain.

She set off the next morning and at long last, on May 14, she crossed the state line and left Georgia behind. She started up the first mountain in North Carolina and the sun beat down upon her neck. She was tired. She raked together a bed of leaves and settled in for a nap; when she woke, she felt a little like Rip Van Winkle.

That afternoon, as another storm approached, she heard a cowbell clanking in the forest and a man calling hogs in the distance. She thought there might be a place to stay nearby, but when she walked down into the gap she didn't see a soul. No homes. No hogs.

She was walking through a part of the world that was full of secrecy and distrustful of outsiders, the broad and beautiful setting for a never-ending game of cat-and-mouse between the people of the hills and the government stiffs. In these secluded hills, a man could scrape out only a meager living through lawful ways. If he wanted to get ahead, he needed more than a few hogs and a rocky plot of corn. The mountains were both a curse and a blessing, though, and the thick woods, tall peaks, and skinny valleys provided natural coverage for an assortment of clandestine entrepreneurialism. Chief among them was moonshining. It started with the water, pure and cold, which bubbled up endlessly out of limestone springs. It was aided by the blue haze that hung low and camouflaged the hickory smoke from the fires that cooked the mash. So out flowed secret streams of illegal moonshine, 100-proof white lightning, in the trunks of jalopies destined for the big cities of the Midwest— Detroit, Chicago, and Indianapolis. The local lawmen tended to look the other way. Cutting stills was impolitic. The state, however, saw opportunity—specifically the opportunity to tax and tax often. And if it couldn't tax, it could handcuff—and thus raged a battle that occasionally sent bullets whizzing through these hollers.

Emma was a teetotaler. She didn't even drink coffee, and she took great pride in that fact, making a point to turn it down outright, a hidden lecture buried in her refusal. But she knew of the battles that had seized the region and she tried to be careful as she plodded through.

She was startled when a man stepped from behind a tree.

Are there any houses around here? she asked.

Not around here, he said.

The man introduced himself as Mr. Parker, and another man walked up to them, Mr. Burch. They told her they had been checking on their hogs, which roamed free in the woods, each wearing a cowbell, and they were camping at a lean-to a few miles away. If she could walk there, she was welcome to stay, they said.

They seemed nice enough. She agreed, and Mr. Burch took her pack and carried it toward the shelter. When they arrived, another man, Mr. Enloe, joined them. They gave Emma straw for a bed and let her dry her wet clothes by their fire.

In the morning, two of the men left after breakfast and said they'd return by dinner, leaving Emma alone with Mr. Burch. She had decided to take the day off to give her aching legs time to recover. They asked her to make cakes out of the stewed potatoes left over from breakfast, so she mixed the potatoes with flour and eggs and fried the loose patties in a skillet over the fire. She'd come to the trail for solidarity with nature, for peace, and here she was, doing chores for a group of men.

That afternoon, the forest warden and game warden stumbled upon Emma and Mr. Burch. They though Emma was Burch's wife. She was embarrassed, but didn't correct them. She didn't want to explain what she was doing out on the trail. She didn't want to talk about why she was walking, or what she had walked away from.

— — — — —

He found her in the dark.

She was walking home from church in Crown City, Ohio, on a chilly night. He rode up beside her on his horse, Dick. Her cousin, Carrie Trowbridge, knew him from town and introduced them.

P. C. Gatewood was the catch of Gallia County, Ohio. He was slender, with a soft tan complexion and short brown hair. He was a strident Republican, and he came from plutocrats—regional royalty, or at least they presented themselves in that fashion. His family owned a furniture factory in Gallipolis. At twenty-six, he was eight years older than Emma, and he seemed worldly, aristocratic even. He had earned a teaching degree from Ohio Northern University, making him one of a handful in the region with a college diploma, and he taught children to read and write at the one-room schoolhouse nearby.

He asked if she wanted a ride and she accepted. He helped her up onto Dick. She had never ridden behind a man before, and as they galloped down the road she could scarcely stay on the horse. There was no way she was going to put her hands around P.C.'s waist.

He carried her home several times that winter, through the barren trees that cast crooked shadows on the hollows, but she never grew bold enough to slide her hands around his body. That wouldn't be proper. One night, she fell off—slid right off the back of the animal. P.C. stopped long enough to give her a hand back on.

Winter turned to spring and P.C. began making more advances. Emma hadn't spent much time thinking about a future with him, but in March he suddenly grew more serious. Out of the blue, he asked her to marry him. For the life of her, she couldn't understand why he was rushing. He seemed to want to get married right away. She wasn't ready. She bided her time and put him off for two months.

They'd come from different lives, raised in close proximity but worlds apart. She'd been born in October 1887, in a puny house near Mercerville, a mile from where the creek forked. The house had a barn, a well, and a terrible view of an ugly bluff, but the children played over the hills. There were twelve in all at the time, and their parents shoved them off to the one-room Cofer School when they didn't have chores at home, which was rarely.

Her father, Hugh Caldwell, was a Civil War veteran, Union tried and true, whose parents had come from Scotland to farm. He was famous for having raised his head above a stone wall in the heat of battle to see where the enemy was. He was wounded later and then lost his bad leg, and after the war he was considered an old reprobate with an affinity for gambling and a taste for whiskey. Her mother, Evelyn Esther Trowbridge, was of British decent, offspring of a clan of Trowbridges who came to America in the 1620s. She was not far removed from Levi Trowbridge, who fought in Capt. Thomas Clark's Derby Company in the Revolutionary War, and with the Green Mountain Boys under General Ethan Allen.

Emma had lived a dozen lives by eighteen. She still bore the scars from the day her sister, Etta, was heating water to wash in a kettle and a spark jumped out of the fire and caught Emma's clothes. Her mother applied medicine with a feather. Emma ate fruit from the blackhaw tree and chased her cousin around the barn. When her family moved to Platform, in Lawrence County, near Guyan Creek, her father intended to build a new house. He set the stone but never got around to erecting the rest. They stayed instead in a log cabin, and her father built an extra bedroom on the front porch. The children slept four to a bed, and in the winter the snow on the clapboard roof would blow in on them and they'd shake the covers before it could melt. They peed off the front porch when their parents weren't looking.

Her mother birthed three more children in that house, making fifteen in all, ten girls and five boys. On hot afternoons, they waded into the creek to get their clothes wet before they took to the fields to hoe corn or plant beans or worm and sucker tobacco or harvest sugar cane and wheat. They'd work until their clothes had dried, then repeat the cycle. Once, when Emma was instructed to plant pumpkins, she grew tired of the monotonous chore and planted handfuls of seeds in each hill. Every plant came up and her little secret was out.

On Sunday mornings, they put on their best clothes and walked a mile to Platform to Sunday school, and after church, the children would climb into the fingers of young trees and ride them to the ground. They hunted wildflowers and climbed all the cliffs they could find, and on one they held firm to a bush and rappelled down its face to peek into a small cave. Once, Emma's older sisters told her she could catch sparrows at the cattle barn if she threw a little salt on their tails. For hours she worked that Sunday, trying to salt the birds' tails.

The children would take a jug of water and set it by a bumblebee nest, then punch the nest. The bees flitted out of the nest and went straight into the jug, and the children plunged their hands into the nest for raw honey.

They went to school just four months a year, due to their farm work, and sometimes that dwindled to two. A gander stood guard outside Guyan Valley School, and when he saw the kids coming he'd stretch out his neck and flap his wings and hiss. Occasionally he'd make contact and bring tears.

In 1900, when Emma was thirteen, her father sold the farm and bought another on the Wiseman's side of Raccoon Creek, a mile above Asbury Methodist Church and a mile below the Wagner post office. They sent the children to Blessing to school, but all were behind in their grades. They tried hard and finally caught up, but the school only went to eighth grade.

When Emma was seventeen, her father fell at work and broke his good leg. Her mother took him to Gallipolis and he was hospitalized for two months. Emma stayed home from school and did the work. She milked the cow before breakfast and did the washing on Saturdays. The boys killed hogs and Emma had to make the sausage, lard, and head cheese. Her mother was surprised that things were in such good order when she returned. Emma had done all the mending, cooking, and cleaning, too.

In 1906, when she was eighteen, she left home for eight weeks to work as a housemaid in Huntington, West Virginia, across the

Emma, third from left, in front of Blessing School in Green Township, around age seventeen. Courtesy Lucy Gatewood Seeds

Ohio River. She hated it and came home as soon as she could. That summer, her cousin Carrie Trowbridge asked her to come and stay with Mrs. Pickett, her grandmother, who lived near Sugar Creek. Mrs. Pickett paid Emma seventy-five cents a week and she was responsible for the milking, washing on the board, ironing, cleaning, shelling corn for the chickens, bringing in coal for the cooking, and washing dishes.

That's when she met P.C.

There she was, away from home, him asking her to marry and her keeping him at arm's length. But he'd had enough of this game of hard-to-get. He threatened to leave, to head west and never come back, if she refused to be his wife. She begrudgingly said yes.

She quit school and collected some clothes and went to her aunt Alice Pickett's house, where Perry was waiting with her uncle, Asa Trowbridge. On May 5, 1907, the two exchanged vows and Emma Caldwell became Mrs. P. C. Gatewood.

They celebrated with a large dinner, then rode in a covered buggy up the Ohio River to Gallipolis and out to her mother's place above Northup, where they spent their honeymoon night in a room fashioned out of bedsheets, before heading up to the little log cabin he owned on a hillside above Sugar Creek.

It wasn't long before the honeymoon was over. P.C. began treating Emma as a possession, demanding she do his work. Mopping, building fences, burning tobacco beds, mixing cement. It wasn't what she had in mind, but she tried hard to make the best of it.

They were married three months before he drew blood.

— — — — —

Standing Indian Mountain jutted from the earth nearly a mile, the highest point on the trail south of the Great Smokies. Emma, after a full day of rest and a good night's sleep on a bed of hay in the

P.C. and Emma Gatewood, shortly after their marriage. Courtesy Lucy Gatewood Seeds

lean-to, saying farewell to the men and pigs, and having a breakfast of leftover potato cakes, pushed forward, canvas Ked in front of canvas Ked, until she crested the mountain in the mid-morning.

The mountain was named by the Cherokee, who told of a great winged creature that made its home here. A bolt of lightning shattered the mountain and killed the creature, but it also struck a warrior, who was turned to stone. The mountain was named on account of a peculiar rock formation that used to jut from the bald precipice and looked very much like a man.

It took her an hour and a half to ascend, and behind her was a superb view of the Georgia Blue Ridge Mountains from which she'd come, through Deep Gap and Muskrat Creek and Sassafras Gap and Bly Gap. She needed to doctor her feet, but it was too early to stop, and even without a map she knew the toughest part of the journey so far was just ahead of her.

After a long trek through Beech Gap and Betty Creek Gap she began to climb Mount Albert, scrambling much of the way over steep rocks, and it was indeed the hardest climb yet in the thirteen days she'd been hiking.

That evening, after twenty miles of walking, she ventured two miles off the trail to find a place to stay. She discovered an empty lean-to at White Oak Forest Camp. The night was cold and she tried to build a fire, but her matches were wet and would not strike. She squirmed into a corner of the shelter and shivered under the blanket until she fell asleep.

She was greeted by rain the next morning, so rather than set off she walked to the game warden's house and introduced herself. The warden's name was Waldroop, and he and his wife drove Emma two miles back to the trail on their way to town. She started off slow, rain falling all day, and she arrived at Wayah Camp at 4:00 PM and built a small fire to dry her clothes. The nearest lean-to had an earthen floor, which was cold, so she heated a long board over the fire and rested atop it for warmth. When the board cooled, she did it again.

She left ten minutes after six the next morning, greeted by the early birds of the Nantahala—a Cherokee word meaning "land of the noonday sun"—a vast and dark forest visited by Spanish conquistador Hernando de Soto in the sixteenth century and the naturalist William Bartram in the eighteenth. When Bartram came through, he "beheld with rapture and astonishment a sublimely awful scene of power and magnificence, a world of mountains piled upon mountains." He continued:

> The mighty cloud now expands its sable wings, extending from North to South, and is driven irresistibly on by the tumultuous winds, spreading his livid wings around the gloomy concave, armed with terrors of thunder and fiery shafts of lightning; now the lofty forests bend low beneath its fury, their limbs and wavy boughs are tossed about and catch hold of each other; the mountains tremble and seem to reel about, and the ancient hills to be shaken to their foundation: the furious storm sweeps along, smoking through the vale and descending from the firmament, and I am deafened by the din of thunder; the tempestuous scene damps my spirits, and my horse sinks under me at the tremendous peals, as I hasten for the plains.

Here walked a new pioneer, her swollen feet inside worn-out tennis shoes, climbing up to Wayah Bald, and up the steps of a stone fire tower built twenty years before by the Civilian Conservation Corps, spinning now, absorbing the breathtaking views of the surrounding range, the world of mountains piled upon mountains, alone, happy.

3

RHODODENDRON AND RATTLESNAKES

The hiking past Wayah Bald was difficult. The trail was unkempt and not well marked. By the time she crossed the Nantahala River on a railroad bridge she was growing hungry, but her supplies were gone. She ventured off the trail and found a small sassafras tree in the forest. She picked the tender young leaves from the tips of its branches and made a salad. Nearby, she found a bunch of wild strawberries. They were tart, but nice.

The path to Wesser Bald had been washed out by the creek and the muck made walking difficult. She stopped at a little trailside store to restock, buying a quart of milk, some cheese crackers, fig bars, two eggs, and a pocketknife. She'd lost her old knife somewhere along the trail.

The next morning, she began her ascent of Swim Bald, which took about three and a half hours, but just before she reached the top, she slipped on a slick boulder, fell, and broke her walking cane. She picked herself up off the rock and checked to see if everything was in order. It was, and she pressed on. She found a new walking stick and crested Cheoah Bald by 10:30 AM. She came down through Locust Cove Gap and Simp Gap and Stecoah Gap and Sweetwater Gap and, growing tired, looked for a place to sleep. There were no shelters, and a tall mountain loomed before her. The sun was fading, so she found a bare spot along the trail, built a fire, and settled in to rest for the night.

She was surrounded by unfamiliar territory, alone in a foreign place, full of curiosity and also dread and fear of the unknown. She hadn't seen another soul on the trail since the men, days before. Most of her routine had been set in the deep solitude of a southern spring, surrounded by a nature very much alive, by chirping birds and buzzing insects, but uninterrupted by human activity. That was about to change.

— — — — — —

The stretch of fertile farmland along the Ohio River in Gallia County was dotted by white wooden houses built snug against the hillsides, the occasional tin-roofed barn beckoning you to CHEW MAIL POUCH TOBACCO. People marked time here by floods and snowstorms, and they kept track of their lineage on the front pages of their Holy Bibles. Their ancestors were French Royalists, and they had been swindled. Five hundred noblemen, artisans, and professionals had bought parcels in Ohio, sight unseen, from a sham company, and they sped west across the Atlantic in January 1790. Upon arrival they learned they owned nothing but paper. Most of them left within two years, but the twenty families that remained etched out a harsh and uncertain living until settlers from Massachusetts and Virginia joined them and set about building a stable community a stone's throw from the river. They called it Gallipolis, "the city of Gauls."

A century later, the town had a newspaper and electric street-cars, a hospital and a library. Trains rolled through daily and steamboats slogged by on the Ohio River and preachers set up big tents in parking lots to holler about temperance.

South of town, in a cabin on Sugar Creek, Emma Gatewood learned she was pregnant with her first child not long before her new husband struck her for the first time. He smacked her with an open hand, and the sharp sting of his palm on her cheek stunned her, frightened her. She thought of leaving him that day and that night and on into the next, but where would she go? She had no paying job, no savings, and her education had ended in the eighth grade. She couldn't return home and be a burden on her mother, who remained busy rearing children.

So she bit her tongue and stayed with P.C.

In October 1908, she delivered her first child, Helen Marie. P.C. wanted boys, and told her as much, so she gave birth again the following year, 1909, and again the child was female. They named her Ruth Estell. Their third child was born in June 1911—finally a boy—and they named him Ernest but took to calling him Monroe.

In the spring of 1913, P.C. bought an eighty-acre farm on Big Creek from his uncle, Bill Gatewood, for $1,000. Emma went to work hauling rocks and suckering tobacco, picking apples and pulling hay and coaxing the cows down off the hill—all while taking care of their growing family. She was a practical woman, a Roosevelt Republican, and knew how to do things for herself. She had a set of books from 1908 full of home remedies and concoctions that would take paint off the door or cure dandruff or kill ants. She had ripped out the page that explained how to ferment grapes to make wine.

When she wasn't working or cooking for P.C. or cleaning the house or taking care of the kids, she'd park herself somewhere out of the way and get lost in a book. She read encyclopedias, but she was particularly fond of classic Greek poetry, quest stories like *The Odyssey* and *The Iliad*, and she read them cover to cover when she could find the time.

Their fourth child, William Anderson, was born in January 1914. The following year, the two eldest girls, Helen and Ruth, started school at Sardis, a one-room schoolhouse on the hill near Crown City, by State Route 553.

Then came Rowena, their fifth child, in 1916, and three months later Emma was pregnant again. A few weeks before she was due to give birth, P.C. assaulted her. He didn't drink or smoke, but he could lose his temper without aid, and he punched her in the face and head so many times that for two weeks she could barely rest it on a pillow. They named the baby Esther Ann.

In December 1918, they bought the Brown farm for $30,000, the place their children would come to think of as home. The farm included a field of fertile bottomland that ran flat as a tabletop from their hillside house to the Ohio River, about a quarter mile away. From the front porch, Emma could see the green hills of West Virginia across the river. The house had four bedrooms upstairs and one down, three covered porches and a basement. An old, defunct piano sat in the parlor, with a horsehair sofa that pulled out into a bed. A Victrola sat on a small table, near the bookshelf. The living room had a heating stove and the kitchen held a cooking stove and a sink with a hand pump that drew water from a cistern. One porch had a swing, and the children's rooms had chamber pots they'd use in the winter. There was a plot large enough for a three-acre garden out front, and Emma woke early each day to tend to it by kerosene lamp. She grew rhubarb, cucumbers, beans, and a healthy patch of morning glories.

They had only $5,000 to put down from the sale of their other farm, which meant there was work to be done between there and comfortable. Emma threw herself into it, and saved until it hurt. The children all worked hard, too. By two years old, they were sweeping floors and gathering eggs. By three they were collecting kindling for the potbellied stove. By four they were washing and drying dishes. By five they knew how to wash their own clothes.

Each morning, P.C. would rise at five and dress and walk to the bottom of the stairs, where he'd pound on the newel post while calling out their names. The kids would jump to their feet from where they slept, four to a bed. The girls swept the house and did the dishes and sometimes helped prepare the meals. After breakfast, they'd all head out into the fields to hoe or pull weeds or pick vegetables or deworm the tobacco plants. The younger children were charged with filling a bucket with lime and walking among the muskmelons and watermelons, sprinkling the mixture on the vines as they went.

To prepare the fields, P.C. hitched a drag to a team of horses to break the earth, and the kids would sometimes climb onto the flat wooden contraption and drag their bare feet in the loamy soil.

Emma went to the fields each day and worked alongside the farmhands, as did all the kids. When the work was done, the children would tear off across the bottoms toward the Ohio River, between their home and the mountains. A few of them could swim to the other side, but most stayed in the shallows, laughing and splashing off the day's dirt. They'd sing "Old Black Joe" and climb inside an old tire and spank each other down the hillside.

At harvest time, they'd pick muskmelons, watermelons, tomatoes, cucumbers, and corn. P.C. took most of it to the Saturday market down in Huntington. The rest they ate or canned or sold at a little vegetable stand by the highway. Muskmelons or a dozen ears of sweet corn for ten cents. Cucumbers for a penny each. Emma canned hundreds of gallons of fruits and vegetables for the summer and winter, and the shelves in the cold underground cellar were lined with scores of half-gallon jars.

They ate everything that came from the earth and wasn't poisonous, from blackberries to persimmons to wild raspberries. They learned that birds and animals don't go hungry, so why should people? So many trees and bushes provided food—hickory nut, beechnut, walnut, honey locust pod, maple syrup, crabapple, mulberry, plum, cherry, huckleberry. Edible plants included dandelions, narrow dock, wild lettuce, white top, clovers, violets, meadow lettuce, poke leaves, and milkweed. And nothing went to waste.

Once in a while the men would kill a fattened hog, and they'd build a fire under a fifty-five-gallon drum full of well water. Late in the day they'd string the hog from a tree and gut it. When the water was hot enough they'd lower the heavy carcass into the drum, then crank it back up and run their sharpened knives over the flesh to remove the coarse hair from the hide. They'd portion the hog and Emma would take the hams, prepare them and smoke them in the smokehouse. She'd take all the meat from the head and cover it in brine in a ceramic crock, sometimes adding a little vinegar, and make hog's head cheese. She'd stuff green peppers with shredded cabbage and dunk them into the brine. It wasn't rare for the kids to eat so much that they became sick.

When she cured the bacon, she'd remove the rind and cut it into small strips and cook it in a heavy pot to render the lard and preserve the skin, which she called cracklings. The children ached for the hog slaughter because it meant their school lunches would include biscuits and homemade jam and fried pork loin.

Emma made apple butter in a giant cauldron over a large fire outside. She put the girls in charge of stirring the fresh, peeled apples constantly with a long wooden paddle and they occasionally got too close and felt the sting of popping hot apple butter on their skin.

She made chicken and dumplings and chicken and noodles and every once in a while, on special occasions, fried chicken. Once every summer a man drove around to the farms with a truck full of various cuts of beef. Emma would peek inside and ask the man about prices. She could never afford much, but sometimes she'd walk away with a chuck roast and she'd make a giant pot of stew. Beef was rare, though—so rare that one of the boys walked into the barn once and bit a cow on the ear to see if it tasted like beef.

She served breakfast at a long table, and P.C. always sat at the head. Sometimes, if the farmhands joined them, there'd be seventeen mouths waiting to be fed. She'd come from the kitchen with large pans of biscuits, bowls of oatmeal and cornmeal mush, and bacon. She served pancakes but refused to flavor her syrup.

When the children needed to relieve themselves, they used the outhouse, which they called "the closet" or "bath with a path." It was a three-seater, and they wiped their behinds with pages torn from the Sears, Roebuck catalog to save money on toilet paper. They walked to school, barefoot sometimes, because they each got just two pairs of twenty-five-cent shoes a year, and they had to make them last.

At Christmas, P.C. would chop down a tree and drag it home. The older children would string popcorn and make ornaments from last year's wrapping paper or the tinfoil from chewing gum or cigarette packages that they found along the road. Their stockings were filled with an orange, a banana, a candy cane, English walnuts, and a new pencil or handkerchief. Most of the larger gifts they shared, including a sled one year and a single pair of roller skates another. Emma sometimes made the girls little dolls with ceramic heads and sawdust stuffing.

P.C. was a thinker, a renaissance man, and his neighbors thought highly of him, even if he overpaid his farmhands. He'd taught school for fifteen years—at the one-room Oak Dale and Waugh Bottom schools—before he quit to run a farm and grow a family, which expanded again in 1920, with the birth of twins, Robert Wilson and Elizabeth Caldwell. He drew blueprints and built a beautiful modern home for his parents on a hillside not far away. He also designed and constructed a new schoolhouse at Swan Creek.

The neighbors knew of his above-average intellect. He'd bought a large tobacco barn for one hundred dollars from a man who lived a mile away and had numbered every board, into the thousands, then disassembled the barn and hauled it down the road and up the hill and to a level patch behind their house where he rebuilt it, nail by nail and board by board. When he finished the project, he climbed to the peak of the aluminum roof and did a handstand while the farmhands cheered at his thin silhouette.

On Sundays, he required the children attend church. They'd pack into a pew at the Methodist church near Swan Creek, where they'd sweat and swat flies for hours while the preacher tried to save their souls from eternal damnation. P.C. made a point of delivering a short sermon to the congregation, himself, when the preacher had finished.

Always, though, just beyond the thin shroud of his respectable public persona, there gurgled a mean streak, and if something set him off, he'd grow wild-eyed and his veins would bulge. His children once watched him beat a stubborn horse half to death with a leather strop. He was prone to administer discipline on his own blood with a briar switch or fire poker or whatever instrument was close at hand.

His madness, in the right moment, wasn't even bound by law. In 1924, a year after Emma delivered their ninth child, P.C. killed a man.

P. C. Gatewood and Hiram Johnson got into an argument one afternoon. The state would charge P.C. with manslaughter and the trial would drag on. Young Monroe, twelve at the time, would testify that Hiram Johnson had fetched his rifle and Monroe had fetched his daddy's for him, and just as Hiram had raised his gun, P.C. had swung his and caught Johnson on the forehead, the approximate site of a fresh wound from an earlier scrap the old man had found himself in. He never regained consciousness and four days later, in the hospital, Hiram died.

Word was that Johnson's widow would not sue P.C. because he'd paid the medical bills and funeral expenses. But a lawyer from Huntington, West Virginia, convinced her to try for a settlement and she won. P.C. was convicted of manslaughter and ordered to pay $50,000. His prison sentence was suspended because he had nine children and a farm to tend to, but the debt was so burdensome that he had to sell half the land. Even then he couldn't make ends meet, and each year it got worse. By the time Dora Louise was born in 1926, and Lucy Eleanor in 1928, P.C. was struggling to keep his farm running. In August 1929, he got a job with the Ohio Township rural school board, hauling pupils from Sugar Creek to Crown City and back for seventy-five dollars a month. He converted an old pickup truck into a makeshift school bus to make the runs. The board hired him again the following year, but in 1932 the contract went to Stanley Swain, who offered to do it for seven dollars less.

The extra income was missed as the Gatewoods inched through the worst of the Great Depression and tried to cope with a drought that had started in the east and raked across the country toward the Great Plains. Crop prices had fallen drastically. That same year, nearly 40 percent of the labor force was out of work. By the following year, more than 40 percent of Ohio factory workers and 67 percent of Ohio construction workers were unemployed, and many of them, with nowhere to turn, were moving from cities like Akron and Toledo and Columbus to the countryside to try to feed their children off the land.

It wasn't unusual for tramps to stop at the house on the hill and ask for food. They all had the same look of desperation. Though she eschewed government handouts, Emma was always generous and invited them to sit on the porch and enjoy a hearty meal. She'd do anything for someone who needed help, and often nursed sick friends back to health. P.C. occasionally let the tramps sleep in his barn if they promised not to smoke. The children sometimes followed the travelers down the highway, and they'd grow old remembering one particular family. The man was driving a dog team, which was pulling a small cart loaded with their possessions. The woman was pregnant, clutching a young child, her feet hanging down off the back.

In 1932, as progressive New York governor Franklin D. Roosevelt chased vulnerable President Herbert Hoover, P.C., a longtime

Republican, switched parties. Emma would have none of it. When the election rolled around, P.C. was in his sickbed, eaten up with ulcers. Pollsters were dispatched to his home to record his vote, but Emma wouldn't let them inside. This event added yet another layer to their discord.

P. C. Gatewood, with the help of his wife and children, held on, but they wouldn't hold the farm through the decade. And he was becoming increasingly difficult to live with.

— — — — — —

Emma trudged on, as May wound down, through lonely woods. She sucked on bouillon cubes as she hiked, and found water where she could. She filled up on wild strawberries—whenever she found a patch, she'd drop her sack and stuff it with as many as she could carry. After a hard climb up Shuckstack Mountain, she discovered a dented trash can lid that had collected a small puddle of rainwater. It was just enough to wet her throat. She cleaned the lid to collect more from the looming rainstorm. There was just enough room on the precipice for a small fire tower, and she made her bed on the porch, propping up several planks to shield her from the strong wind.

The next afternoon, she ran into a man and woman, the first couple she'd seen on the trail. She was out of food, and after she explained what she was doing, the day hikers felt sorry for her and divided their supplies. She made it to Spence Camp in a downpour, a rain so hard she couldn't light a fire. It was only 4:00 PM, but she hung up her wet clothes and climbed into the lean-to and tried to sleep, wet as she was.

She wasn't down long when a man appeared out of the woods. He introduced himself as Lionel Edna and said he had been painting trail blazes, white, two inches by six inches long, on trees along the path. He fixed himself supper as they chatted, then climbed into his sleeping bag on the opposite side of the shelter. They talked a while before drifting off.

She left early the next morning and the wind had picked up, giant gusts that nearly blew her down. The weather was odd, she thought, for May in the South. The rain started at 11:00 and she decided to call it a day when she reached a shelter around 2:00 PM. She found some dry wood and built a fire and washed and dried her clothes.

The following afternoon, she trudged into Newfound Gap, near the center of the Great Smoky Mountains National Park, and into the strangest scene she'd seen so far. There were people everywhere at the popular park, including about a dozen nuns who were slapping each other on the back and acting like teenagers. She watched one of them climb onto a wall and shout and jump off, as the rest of them laughed. They were giddy, having fun and playing around a stone monument built to honor the Rockefellers.

Emma noticed a bus stop nearby. Her shoes were about ruined, and hiking through all this rain without a raincoat was miserable, so she reckoned she could use a few supplies. Gatlinburg, Tennessee, wasn't far, so she decided she'd catch the bus. Just then, one of the nuns approached and asked if she could take a picture of Emma.

She bought shoes and a raincoat and got a bite to eat in Gatlinburg, then tried to hitchhike back to the trail, but nobody would stop. She checked into a motel instead.

She caught the bus the next morning and got back on the trail by 8:00 AM, hiking quickly to break in her new sneakers. A heavy fog settled over the Smoky Mountains that evening and a chill set in, so Emma heated smooth stones in the fire and slept atop them to keep her back warm.

She made it to the edge of the Smoky Mountain National Park, near the line separating North Carolina and Tennessee, the following day, and she fell in love with the fields of rhododendron and laurel that seemed to be growing everywhere she looked. She lost the trail once and asked some boys to point her in the right direction. When she found the trail in the rain, it had been plowed up. The muck from the tilled field clung to her shoes and the walk through the field was staggering. On the other side, as she walked down an abandoned buggy road, she found herself in a tunnel through the tall rhododendron. It was dark and eerie and, as the rain fell into the tunnel, quite beautiful.

She made it into Hot Springs, North Carolina, on May 28, after an arduous uphill climb. The little town on the French Broad River whispered of the past. In 1914, during World War I, the owner of a resort called the Mountain Park Hotel had struck a deal with the War Department to house prisoners of war there. By train came 2,200 Germans, four times the population of the town. They were mostly passengers, officers, and crew members from the world's largest ship, the *Vaterland*, which had taken cover in an American port when Great Britain had declared war on Germany.

They were no ordinary prisoners of war. The men wore suits and ties and the women were fantastic dressmakers. They set about building a village on the hotel lawn using driftwood and scrap lumber. They built a chapel from flattened Prince Albert Tobacco tins. The townspeople developed friendships with the enemy aliens, and each Sunday afternoon they sat together for a concert from the prisoner orchestra. After the war, the prisoners from what had been the largest internment camp in the United States were transported to Fort Oglethorpe, in Georgia, where Emma had started her journey. But many of them had found their nineteen months of captivity so enjoyable that they returned with their families and settled in Hot Springs.

Emma sensed that brotherly love. The folks in the area were awfully nice, and just about everybody she bumped into insisted on feeding her and giving her something to drink. One woman gave her a glass of buttermilk and a piece of cake, her first on the trail, and she enjoyed it. She heard the locusts sawing for the first time all year. On May 29, she came upon a small store and intended to buy some food for the desolate walk ahead. All the store had was a can of black beans and a box of raw prunes. She bought them anyway, and chewed the dry, hard prunes all afternoon until they were gone.

The sun was hot as she made her way up Turkey Bald Mountain. The climb was slow and Emma was lost in her thoughts when she heard something strange. It sounded like some kind of bird at first, a low sort of hiss, and she kept walking, unafraid, until she felt something strike the leg of her dungarees. She glanced down and there beside the trail was a rattlesnake, coiled and ready to strike again. She slammed the tip of her walking stick toward the snake and jumped sideways. She darted by, her adrenaline surging, her ribs rising with each short, sharp breath. The snake stayed coiled and Emma was soon yards past it, thankful, reminded of the danger of a single misstep.

4

WILD DOGS

She'd been gone nearly a month.

Emma's children hadn't heard from her, had no idea where she was or what she was doing, but not one of them was worried. Their mama was raw-boned and sturdy, and despite her absence, they knew she'd be all right, whatever her ambitions. It wasn't rare for her to be gone for long stretches, so if they gave her disappearance a passing thought, it did not dwell in their memories.

She zigzagged between North Carolina and Tennessee, thirsty, sore, tired, over roads of cut stone and up mountainsides steep and tall, sleeping outdoors more often than in, giving herself to the wilderness, planting a crop of memories, exploring the world and her own mind, writing in her little notebook of the challenges and rewards, the wild dogs that came in the night, the cozy fire that made a campsite more cheerful, the magic of campers who shared their sausage sandwiches across picnic tables.

"My feet are sore," she would write.

"I did not find any water," she would write.

"I kept a fire for company as well as protection," she would write.

"When I could not locate the trail after an hour, I was so near out of food," she would write.

Occasionally, when she'd slip off the path, the woman who wouldn't let a passing tramp go hungry back home in Ohio now gladly accepted invitations to rest or eat from the members of the long, linear neighborhood that was slowly, hiker by hiker, getting acquainted with the new Appalachian Trail.

— — — — — —

The trail itself was the product of a dreamer, a man named Benton MacKaye. He said he had been inspired during a six-week hiking trip after graduating from Harvard, when he stood on Vermont's Stratton Mountain and imagined a ridge-top trail running through wilderness across the entire distance of the range.

In 1921, when the idea had fermented, some friends convinced him to describe his vision in an article for the *Journal of the American Institute of Architects*. MacKaye wrote that the purpose of the trail would be to "extend the primeval environment and to set bounds to the metropolitan environment," providing a grand natural backbone accessible by those packed into cities along the Eastern Seaboard. After the article was published, MacKaye led a concerted effort to involve hiking clubs, lawyers, and others who might help bring his plan to fruition. Hundreds contributed, blazing and mapping sections, searching through property and tax records in county courthouses, angling to cobble together and preserve for the public the longest continuous walking path in the world.

Ten years later, nearly half the trail had been marked—but mostly in the Northeast, where many trails had long been established and hiking communities had a history. Myron Avery, a young lawyer and early visionary who took the reins, helped organize hiking clubs and plan undeveloped sections. Avery became chairman of the fledgling Appalachian Trail Conference in 1931, and by the group's meeting in 1937 in Gatlinburg, Tennessee, the trail was nearly finished. Avery knew even then, though, that the A.T. would "never be completed." It would shift and bend and be subjected to endless rerouting and relocation, as if it had a life of its own. The timing of the completion was perfect, and it's quite possible the trail might not have existed if the plan had been delayed.

At the beginning of the twentieth century, the United States had just one hundred miles of paved highways. But by the 1930s, cities had begun to spill outward, like a spreading blot, and roads that had been designed for horses and buggies were quickly becoming obsolete. Maybe those early A.T. volunteers felt the need for expediency as their country transformed quickly, as the population grew, as the American automobile industry sped forward at an unprecedented rate.

The very same year of the trail conservancy meeting in Gatlinburg, in fact, the federal Public Works Administration signed a check for more than $29 million and the federal Reconstruction Finance Corporation bought nearly $41 million in revenue bonds, and 10,000 men began working day and night to move 26 million tons of earth and stone and pour 4.3 million square yards of reinforced concrete to create two steady, even, parallel lanes that ran the length of Pennsylvania—including more than 114 new bridges, with acceleration lanes and paved shoulders—bisecting the state east to west. *Popular Mechanics* would call the Penn Turnpike "America's first highway on which full performance of today's automobiles can be realized."

The big road was born.

It's ironic, perhaps, but the new expressway's conceptual father was the same man who thought up the Appalachian Trail: Benton MacKaye. A few years after his article on the "primeval environment" that stretched from north to south, MacKaye, in an article in the *New Republic*, envisioned a "highway completely free of horses, carriages, pedestrians, town, grade crossings; a highway built for the motorist and kept free from every encroachment, except the filling stations and restaurants necessary for his convenience."

Two years later, as the small army of trail blazers and pioneers worked to connect and maintain a footpath through a streak of American wilderness, President Franklin D. Roosevelt was already planning ways to absorb millions of soldiers, soon to engage fully in World War II, back into the nation's economy once the last bullet had been fired. And he saw a national system of highways that connected the country's major cities and spliced together rural agriculture centers as a possible solution. Planners immediately started charting a proposal to build or expand nearly forty thousand miles of road. By 1939, when Ford Motor Co.'s "The Road of Tomorrow" and General Motors' "Highways and Horizons" exhibits opened at the New York World's Fair, the American public was salivating over high-speed roadways.

"Since the beginning of civilization, transportation has been the key to man's progress—his prosperity—his happiness," said a narrator at the GM exhibit, which was said to feature the new and improved American city of 1960, with tangles of expressways lined with sleek cars and trucks. "With the fast, safely designed highways of 1960 . . . thrilling scenic feasts of great and beautiful country may now be explored."

When Dwight D. Eisenhower took office in 1953, one of his first items of business was to see about building better highways. "Our cities still conform too rigidly to the patterns, customs, and practices of fifty years ago," he wrote. "Each year we add hundreds of thousands of new automobiles to our vehicular population, but our road systems do not keep pace with the need."

Eisenhower thought the American road system was decent but had been designed based on "terrain, existing Indian trails, cattle trails, and arbitrary section lines," and that it "has never been completely overhauled or planned to satisfy the needs of ten years ahead." On Eisenhower's behalf, at a meeting in the Adirondacks of the governors of the forty-eight states, Vice President Richard Nixon despaired over the nearly 40,000 people killed and 1.3 million injured on roads annually, the "billions of hours lost" to traffic jams and detours, and the traffic-related civil suits clogging courts. Then he shocked the room. He called for a $50 billion federal highway program spread over ten years.

On October 23 of the same year, in Emma Gatewood's home state of Ohio, the first concrete was poured for a new $336 million cross-state turnpike. The state had acquired fifty-six hundred parcels of land it needed for right-of-way and went to work building a highway divided by a fifty-six-foot depressed median. It would feature paved shoulders, fifteen well-lit traffic interchanges, sixteen service plazas, tollbooths, and an ambulance service. "You really will be able to see where you're going as the minimum sight distance is 900 feet," gushed the *Columbus Dispatch*. "There are no steep hills, because the maximum upgrade is 2 percent and the maximum downgrade 3.2 percent. You won't have to slow down from maximum speed limits—65 miles an hour for cars and 55 for trucks—when you drive around curves, they're that gentle."

Two years later, the ribbons of road stretched from Pennsylvania in the east to Indiana in the west, over rivers and streams, across swampland and rolling hills. Joined with the Penn Turnpike, the road totaled 611 miles from Philadelphia to Indianapolis. So exciting was the new highway that the people of Ohio began to gather on overpasses to watch the speeding cars wend their way along the smooth pavement.

The future of America had arrived, and it was riding on a 322-cubic-inch V-8 with an automatic transmission. By 1955, Americans owned sixty-two million vehicles. By June, when Emma Gatewood was a month into her hike, the auto industry was on pace for a banner year behind presidents such as Tex Colbert and Henry Ford II. Chevrolet had set a six-month record, registering 756,317 new cars. The national magazines were filled with color pictures of the new '56 models, the Studebaker, the Chrysler, the Cadillac, the Buick Dynaflow, with the sweep-ahead styling and the sizzle to match, which "gets going from a standing start like a lark leaving the nest, with not a hint of hesitation between take-hold and take-off." Every car off the line in Detroit was bigger than the last. Fins grew, and engines added horses. The number of two-car families was expected to jump by three million within five years, to a total of 7.5 million, which was attributed to the trend of suburban living. Some sixteen million "one-car wives" remained marooned in the suburbs, but that would soon change. Advertisements for Old Crow bourbon and the Stetson Playboy were surrounded by those for Quaker State Motor Oil and B. F. Goodrich tires.

The rise of the car in the 1950s was accompanied by the rise of television. At the beginning of the decade, only 9 percent of American households had a TV set. More than half had one by 1954, and 86 percent would own one by the end of the decade. Americans began to experience life not by the soles of their feet, but by the seat of their pants.

And along came a startling discovery. In March 1955, two months before Emma set out, a convention of family doctors assembled in Los Angeles to talk about a new generation of surprisingly lethargic children. Two emissaries from the athletic world broke the news: American young people are forgetting how to walk.

So said University of California football coach Lynn "Pappy" Waldorf and US Olympic trainer Eddie Wojecki in the keynote address to the seventh annual assembly of the American Academy of General Practice. Children, the men testified, would rather jump into a car to go a block than walk. And shockingly, the trend had already produced conspicuous changes in the physiques of kids.

The men both spoke of the sudden need to strengthen rather than loosen the muscles of athletes. They ascribed the change to a severe decrease in walking brought about by the habitual use of cars. And they pointed to a simultaneous decline in hiking.

America, it seemed, was at a turning point. When given a choice, Americans preferred to grab the car keys. Streets and cities were being designed for the automobile, rather than the pedestrian. This should have come as no surprise.

Henry David Thoreau predicted as much ninety-three years before Emma's journey, in June 1862, when *Atlantic Monthly* published one of Thoreau's essays, called "Walking."

At present, in this vicinity, the best part of the land is not private property; the landscape is not owned, and the walker enjoys comparative freedom. But possibly the day will come when it will be partitioned off into so-called pleasure-grounds, in which a few will take a narrow and exclusive pleasure only, when fences shall be multiplied, and man-traps and other engines invented to confine men to the public road, and walking over the surface of God's earth shall be construed to mean trespassing on some gentleman's grounds. To enjoy a thing exclusively is commonly to exclude yourself from the true enjoyment of it. Let us improve our opportunities, then, before the evil days are upon us.

Anthropologists estimate that early man walked twenty miles a day. Mental and physical benefits have been attributed to walking as far back as ancient times. The Roman writer Pliny the Elder (23–79 AD) described walking as one of the "Medicines of the Will." Hippocrates, the Greek physician, called walking "man's best medicine" and prescribed walks to treat emotional problems, hallucinations, and digestive disorders. Aristotle lectured while strolling. Through the centuries, the best thinkers, writers, and poets have preached the virtues of walking. Leonardo da Vinci designed elevated streets to protect walkers from cart traffic. Johann Sebastian Bach once walked two hundred miles to hear a master play the organ.

William Wordsworth was said to have walked 180,000 miles in his lifetime. Charles Dickens captured the ecstasy of near-madness and insomnia in the essay "Night Walks" and once said, "The sum of the whole is this: Walk and be happy; Walk and be healthy." Robert Louis Stevenson wrote of "the great fellowship of the Open Road" and the "brief but priceless meetings which only trampers know." Friedrich Wilhelm Nietzsche said, "Only those thoughts that come by walking have any value."

More recently, writers who knew the benefits of striking out excoriated the apathetic public, over and over again, for its laziness.

"Of course, people still walk," wrote a journalist in *Saturday Night* magazine in 1912. "That is, they shuffle along on their own pins from the door to the street car or taxi-cab. . . . But real walking . . . is as extinct as the dodo."

"They say they haven't time to walk—and wait fifteen minutes for a bus to carry them an eighth of a mile," wrote Edmund Lester Pearson in 1925. "They pretend that they are rushed, very busy, very energetic; the fact is, they are lazy. A few quaint persons—boys chiefly—ride bicycles."

"But to dyed-in-the-wool walk-lovers the car has proved a calamity . . . because unless we be strong as steel, our lazy and baser natures yield to the temptation of time-saving when a ride is offered us," wrote Mary Magennis in 1931.

Thoreau's "evil days" had arrived, and the country, keys in hand, was making a dramatic move from feet to tires. The resulting death toll was astounding. By 1934, as the road-building programs gained steam, it was expected that two thousand pedestrians would be killed and eight thousand more injured. Fifteen years later, those numbers had skyrocketed. Cars were killing nearly thirty people a day and injuring seven hundred. A journalist for the *Saturday Evening Post* called it "a feud" between man and automobile. The pedestrian, he wrote, "literally would be safer on a lion-infested African veldt or in man-eating tiger territory than he is crossing a downtown street at dusk."

And at that moment, among the confluence of mechanical engineering and highway building, the Appalachian Trail—the People's Path—was fully blazed and opened to the public. You could set out for a day or a week or a month and lose yourself in the wilderness.

A man named Harold Allen summarized its appeal:

Remote for detachment,
narrow for chosen company,
winding for leisure,
lonely for contemplation,
the Trail leads not merely north and south
but upward to the body, mind and soul of man.

In 1948, Earl V. Shaffer became the first person to hike its entirety in a single trip, the first thru-hiker, and when he was finished, he wrote: "Already it seemed like a vivid dream, through sunshine, shadow, and rain—Already I knew that many times I would want to be back again—On the cloud-high hills where the whole world lies below and far away—By the wind-worn cairn where admiring eyes first welcome newborn day—To walk once more where the white clouds sail, far from the city clutter—And drink a toast to the Long High Trail in clear, cold mountain water."

— — — — —

She came down out of Carver's Gap, near Tennessee's Roan Mountain, on June 4, and she was having no luck finding a place to stay. It seemed the bigger the house, the less likely she would be welcome. One woman was terribly snooty and acted as though she was insulted that Emma had even come to her door. Tired of searching for charity, she checked into a motel on the highway. She washed her hair and some clothes, took a welcome shower, and got a good night's sleep on a soft bed.

The next day's hike was nearly all on paved road and she grew tired quickly. When she could go no farther, she stopped at a little house to ask if she could rest a while on the porch. The man who answered thought she was a government agent who had come to spy on them. He stayed inside with the door latched and asked her all sorts of crazy questions through the screen. She tried to explain who she was and what she was doing, but the man was still suspicious. He asked her if she was with the FBI. When she realized she was making no progress, she stepped off the porch and walked on and finally found a family with seven sons, all at home, who let her stay the night.

She left at a quarter to six the next morning and followed the trail up an Appalachian gorge carved out by the swift waters of Laurel Fork. At the end of the gorge, past eastern hemlocks and sycamore trees, she found a majestic waterfall, the most beautiful she'd ever seen, cascading over moss-covered stone.

She pressed on toward Hampton, Tennessee, but she'd run out of water by the time she reached Watauga Dam, the second tallest of all the Tennessee Valley Authority dams. She asked a man there, standing in front of the sixty-four-hundred-acre lake, for drinking water, but he said there was none around. Emma didn't seem to mind, though. "A very nice looking man he was, too," she wrote in her notebook when she stopped to drink from a spring. She slept that night atop the mountain, and the wild dogs came back, so she built a fire for protection. She stayed awake most of the night, worrying about whether it would rain.

On June 8, a storm moved over the mountains and brought with it rain and sleet and intense cold. Emma put on most of the clothes she had, including three coats, and walked as quickly as she could,

but she couldn't get warm. The trail was lousy with nettles and brush and the hike was miserable, but she finally crossed the state line, into Virginia, and into the little town of Damascus. It was a place that would become known as Trail Town, USA, in part due to its kindness to A.T. hikers, but on that day, when she needed shelter most, she was turned away from a motel. Soaked as she was, they wouldn't keep her. She walked three more blocks and found a cabin for rent, and it was fine. She had privacy, anyway, and she wouldn't be a bother to anyone. She washed some of her clothes and that night, celebrating the fact that she crossed another state line, her third so far, she sat down and treated herself to a delicious supper of steak.

5

HOW'D YOU GET IN HERE?

JUNE 9–22, 1955

She couldn't keep a secret forever.

She had hiked through Jefferson National Forest, then through a long stretch where the trail was torn up from manganese mining, then, nearing Groseclose, Virginia, she found a section flush with peach trees and apple trees and ate her fill, sweet juice on her lips. She had been turned away again at a snooty motel, and had seen a large black-and-yellow butterfly near Goldbond, Virginia, and had found a big white goose feather at the very top of Sinking Creek Mountain. She had stayed the night with Mr. and Mrs. Ed Pugh, and Mr. and Mrs. Hash Burton, and Mr. Lou Oliver, and Mr. and Mrs. Taylor of Pine Ridge, and Dr. and Mrs. Harry Semones, who enjoyed her stories about the trail so much that they kept her up past bedtime.

So it was that on the afternoon of June 20, a Sunday, Emma met a man at a gas station and let slip what she was doing, where she was going. The next day, as she approached Black Horse Gap, she sat down a few yards away from the road, on the edge of the forest, to eat a snack. A car stopped in front of her and the driver pulled onto the shoulder. Two men climbed out, well dressed, and walked toward her. The first introduced himself as Preston Leech, a photographer from Roanoke, Virginia, and the second said he was Frank E. Callahan. They were both trail club members who had

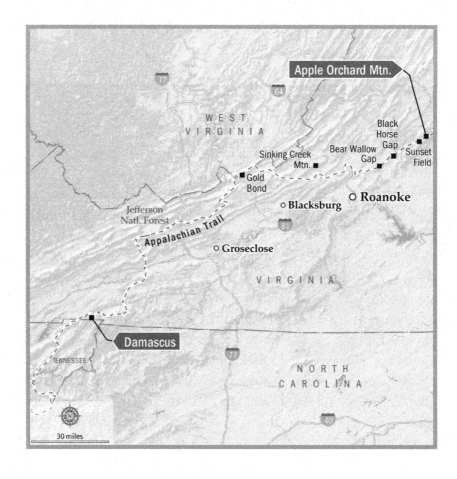

heard about her journey and spent the afternoon trying to track her down. They were overjoyed to finally find her.

They told her they wanted to tell her story, that what she was doing was simply amazing. The exposure would be great for the trail, and people around there would love it.

She wasn't sure. She still hadn't sent word home to her family. Besides, someone might read about her and get the idea to harm her, or take advantage of an old lady. She told them no, that she wouldn't cooperate, but they didn't let up. They convinced her to stay the night at Callahan's cabin near the trail. They took her pack and loaded it into the car, as insurance, and she set off to hike the final ten miles over the mountains to Bear Wallow Gap, where they picked her up and drove her to the cabin. The game warden, J. W. Luck, joined them for dinner, which Callahan spooned from tin cans onto plates.

It was 10:00 PM on the forty-eighth day of her journey when she finally gave in.

Leech fetched his camera. Emma sat up straight, tucked her right hand into her left, and smiled through false teeth.

That night, she jotted in her diary. "I finally was found by the newspaper," she wrote.

The next morning, a headline ran in the *Roanoke Times*.

OHIO WOMAN, 67, HIKING 2,050 MILES ON APPY TRAIL
The prospect of a 2,050-mile hike over mountain trails would cause many a hardy soul to cringe. A 67-year-old great-grandmother from Gallipolis, Ohio, enjoys it.

Mrs. Emma Gatewood, who was in Botetourt County yesterday, is hiking the Appalachian Trail from Georgia to Maine.

She did 20 miles from Cloverdale to Bear Wallow Gap yesterday—in tennis shoes.

Frank Callahan and Preston Leech of the local Appalachian Trail Club met the energetic lady at Black Horse Gap
yesterday afternoon after Blue Ridge Parkway rangers had
reported her whereabouts.

The widowed mother of 11 children, Mrs. Gatewood
spent the winter in California where she decided to travel
the 2,050-mile trail, which follows mountain ranges up the
eastern seaboard. She flew to Atlanta, Ga., and set foot on
the trail at Mt. Oglethorpe, Ga., May 3. End of the trek will
be the northern terminus at Mt. Katahdin, Me.

Modestly reluctant to discuss her plans, Mrs. Gatewood
travels light, said Callahan and Leech. All her belongings
are carried in a sack. She refuses all transportation offers
along the trail but she will accept rides to nearby towns if
she is taken back to the trail where she left it.

The Ohio housewife has 26 grandchildren and two
great-grandchildren.

Today she plans to move from the Peaks of Otter area
north to the James River.

"Uphill walking is easier than going down," she declared.

The news was out. She didn't know it then, but the story—her
story—would soon sweep the nation. She'd be mentioned in newspaper columns from Los Angeles to New York. Television shows
would clamor for her time. As word spread like wood smoke, most
towns she walked through, and even those she didn't, would send
a reporter to intercept her and ask her questions about how she'd
done it, how she was feeling, why she had begun. They'd call her
Grandma Gatewood, and her name would be heard on the street
corners and in the halls of the United States Congress.

That morning, though, it was one measly article in one local
newspaper. Still, she figured it was time to finally let her family

know what she was doing. She picked up a few postcards from the nearest store and dropped them in the mail. When she first left, she had told her children she was going on a walk. Now they'd know what she meant.

— — — — — —

The trail was designed to have no end, a wild place on which to be comfortably lost for as long as one desired. In those early days, nobody fathomed walking the thing from beginning to end in one go. Section hikes, yes. Day hikes, too. But losing yourself for five months, measuring your body against the earth, fingering the edge of mental and physical endurance, wasn't the point. The trail was to be considered in sections, like a cow is divided into cuts of beef. Even if you sample every slice, to eat the entire beast in a single sitting was not the point. Before 1948, it wasn't even considered possible.

How long would it take? What equipment would one need? What maps? Where and when should one start? These were the unknowns, but the human spirit has a way of answering questions. The first came in the form of a man trying to shake his demons.

Earl Shaffer came home from World War II "confused and depressed," he wrote. He had lost a close friend in the war, some-one with whom he had shared a desire to hike the A.T. Like Emma Gatewood, he began considering the hike again after an article in a magazine, *Outdoor Life*, sparked his interest. The strong hiker found a plethora of obstacles: overgrowth, downed trees blocking the path, rough stretches where the trail wasn't marked. Eleven years after its completion, whole sections of the trail seemed abandoned, forgotten.

He sent a postcard to a meeting of the Appalachian Trail Con-ference from Holmes, New York.

The flowers bloom, the songbirds sing
And though it sun or rain
I walk the mountain tops with Spring
From Georgia north to Maine.

The postcard was the first the A.T.C. volunteers had ever heard from Shaffer, and when he finished at Mount Katahdin, some doubted the claim until he showed slides, his journal, and talked about the trail in detail. The *Appalachian Trailway News* ran a small blurb headlined "Continuous Trip over Trail" on the back page, but his hike brought much attention. He was interviewed by the newspaper and got the attention of *National Geographic*, which sent a reporter to hike the trail. The path was in close proximity to half a dozen of the country's biggest cities and nearly half the population of the United States, but before Shaffer, few even knew it existed. The attention helped.

It took three years for someone to repeat Shaffer's achievement. A bearded, twenty-four-year-old Eagle Scout named Gene Espy came through in 1951, but he didn't know he was only the second person to thru-hike until he was shown a newspaper clipping that confirmed it. He assumed many had done it before. Chester Dziengielewski and Martin Papendick became the first to hike the north-to-south route, from Maine to Georgia. In 1952, George Miller became the fifth thru-hiker, at age seventy-two. The first woman to hike the full trail in sections was Mary Kilpatrick, who finished the last part in 1939.

Then there was an enigma. In 1952, hikers along the A.T. reported meeting a couple called Dick Lamb and Mildred. Many assumed the two were married and took to referring to Mildred as Mildred Lamb. In fact, she was Mildred Lisette Norman, an American pacifist, vegetarian, and peace activist who had set out with a friend, Dick, to take the long journey. She eschewed folding money and carried very few supplies, and would later become known as Peace Pilgrim, speaking at churches and universities through the American conflicts in Korea and Vietnam. She and Dick hiked north to the Susquehanna River, then took a bus to Maine and hiked from Mount Katahdin south.

No hiker received all that much attention, though, because independent reports on their progress were either nonexistent or sporadic. Many of them would later write books and communicate regularly with others who planned to thru-hike. But there wasn't exactly an organized system for accountability in those days. The ATC, which was the only outfit interested in paying close attention to trail accomplishments, tended to take people at their word. And that required relying on hikers to both report their trips, and report them accurately.

Besides that, Americans weren't all that interested. Or maybe they were distracted. World War II was over. The Korean War came to a close in 1953. But as soon as soldiers returned, the United States found itself locked in the Cold War, racing Soviet Russia toward the H-bomb. The news of H-bomb developments deeply impacted Americans, who found themselves discussing nuclear fallout and megatons and the genetic consequences of radioactivity at the dinner table.

On March 1, 1954, the United States launched its latest H-bomb on the atoll of Bikini, in the Pacific. The navy had marked off thirty thousand square miles as a danger zone that no ship was allowed to enter.

One made it through, however. A crew of Japanese fishermen aboard a boat called the *Lucky Dragon* were pulling in their nets when the bomb exploded. One of the men gave a captivating, awful account.

"We saw strange sparkles and flashes of fire as bright as the sun itself," the fisherman told the press. "The sky glowed fiery red and yellow. The glow went on for several minutes . . . and then the yellow seemed to fade away. It left a dull red, like a piece of iron cooling in the air. The blast came five minutes later, the sound of many thunders rolled into one. Next we saw a pyramid-shaped cloud rising and the sky began to cloud over most curiously."

A few hours later a fine ash began to fall on the crew of the *Lucky Dragon*, eighty miles from the test site, who continued pulling in nets until the hold was full. They returned to Japan two weeks later complaining of burns, nausea, and bleeding from the gums. By then the radioactive catch, some 16,500 pounds of tuna, had been sold to markets across the country, causing mass panic and raising hostile anti-American sentiment among the Japanese. In September, the crew's radio operator died, becoming the first Japanese victim of a hydrogen bomb.

The unprecedented destructiveness of the brand-new H-bomb was finally on full display, and it horrified the world. If a hydrogen bomb could do that to fishermen eighty miles away, what could it do to Manhattan? Or London? Or Tokyo?

Headlines in England cried: CALL OFF THAT BOMB. Winston Churchill foresaw a "peace of mutual terror." Nikita S. Khrushchev, the First Secretary of the Soviet Communist Party, said, "We outstripped the capitalist class and created the hydrogen bomb before them. They think they can intimidate us. But nothing can frighten us, because if they know what a bomb means, so do we."

At every turn, the United States, with its new destructive technology, was on the cusp of conflict with worldwide implications.

By 1955, the government was ramping up efforts to encourage Americans to prepare for fire from the sky. The Atomic Energy Commission built a million-dollar village, called "Survival City, U.S.A.," in the Nevada desert, and stocked it with the furniture and appliances and mannequins to represent a typical American home. Then, on national television, the village was bombed. The furniture was splintered and the dummies were burned, but the dogs and mice inside deep, concrete bomb shelters were spared, prompting an official with the Federal Civil Defense Administration to say the only shot at American survival was to "dig in or get out."

It wasn't just the Communist bombs Americans were afraid of. It was Communists themselves. The world had been divided after World War II, with Russia on one side and the United States on the other. And by 1955, the fear of Communism in America was intense. The newspapers were filled with stories of spy rings that stole state secrets and agents who had infiltrated government bureaus. The president had ordered chiefs of government bureaus to fire employees whose loyalty was in reasonable doubt and congressional committees were set up to determine the extent of Communist influence in the military and private industry. Libraries banned Communist literature. Colleges demanded loyalty oaths from professors. Some 20 million Americans, more than a tenth of the 166 million US citizens, were subjected to federal security investigations.

On Communism's trail was Wisconsin senator Joseph McCarthy, who had charged in 1950 that the US State Department was a nest of Communists and subversives. By 1954, the strong-necked, emotional politician was the most controversial figure in Washington and a new word had made its debut: McCarthyism. To some he was a fearless patriot, to others a dangerous charlatan. To all observers, he was on the edge of astonishing political power—until he was censured by the US Senate.

With the country buzzing about Communism, the Supreme Court had set the course for another period of disruption and civil unrest when, in May 1954, it ruled that "Separate education facilities are inherently unequal," ending racial segregation in public schools. The ruling touched off praise and anguish.

"Little by little we move toward a more perfect democracy," read an editorial in the *New York Times*.

"The Court has blatantly ignored all law and precedent," said Georgia governor Herman Talmadge. "Georgia will not comply."

The ruling had the largest impact on the states along the Appalachian Trail, especially in the South. School segregation was required in seventeen states at the time of the ruling, and six of those (Georgia, Maryland, North Carolina, Tennessee, Virginia, and West Virginia) were home to the A.T. Four others (Alabama, Delaware, Kentucky, and South Carolina) were close to the trail. In White Sulphur Springs, West Virginia, not far from the trail, three hundred white students held a strike when about twenty-five black students tried to attend school in September 1954. That evening, hundreds of white adults met and voted to remove from class any black students who came to school the next day. None did, but the revolt began to spread, to Milford, Delaware; and Baltimore, Maryland; and Washington, DC.

The other shocking story of the period was the rapid rise in juvenile crime. Headlines in New York screamed about the "Teen-Age Thrill Killers," a band of four boys from respectable Brooklyn homes who killed a man, beat another up and dumped him in the East River, horsewhipped two girls, and set another man on fire.

Across the country, killer kids made news. A twelve-year-old basketball player from Detroit killed another after a game. A seventeen-year-old from Toledo raped and killed a girl. A fourteen-year-old babysitter in Des Moines killed an eight-year-old because he wouldn't stay in bed. The national crime rate for boys and girls under eighteen had jumped 8 percent between 1953 and 1954.

The spree was cause for great concern, and adults found social forces to blame, even two years before anyone had heard of a boy named Elvis Presley: broken homes, television crime programs, comic books, tensions over the threat of war. One other motivator was blamed: inadequate recreation.

— — — — — —

She left Sunset Field, near Roanoke, Virginia, at 5:30 AM and had a difficult time following the trail. Much of it was overgrown, and the blazes were hard to see. She was surprised when the trail led directly to a large woven-wire fence. Beyond it was a huge metal apparatus she didn't recognize. The trail marks stopped, and she couldn't decide where she had gone wrong. She walked along the fence a way and came to a shorter barbed-wire fence, so she climbed through, being careful not to snag her trousers. She came out on a slag road and followed it down to the highway, then found the trail again. She climbed through two more barbed-wire fences, thinking it was odd, but pressing on nonetheless.

Then she saw them. A dozen young men came marching toward her in a tight group, staring at her as if she were a ghost.

Where's the Appalachian Trail? she called out.

One of the men—she took him to be an officer—stepped out of the group and approached her.

You were supposed to take the parkway, he said.

Well, what're those marks for? she asked.

That was the old trail, he said.

She didn't know it, but the year before, the Air Defense Command had established a radar station called Bedford AFS atop Apple Orchard Mountain, one cog in a deployment of dozens of mobile radar stations around the perimeter of the country. It was a massive security effort ten years into the Cold War. The squadron stationed atop the mountain was charged with spotting unidentified planes on the radar and guiding interceptor aircraft toward the intruders.

The men watched the skies, but not so much the ground. Now they surrounded Ms. Emma Gatewood of Gallia County, Ohio, and they stood in shock.

Thank you, she said.

She turned and headed for the gate. The men were silent. As she approached, the guard came out of the shack rubbing his eyes, as if he'd been asleep.

How'd you get in here? he drawled in a hoarse voice.

I crawled through a few barbed-wire fences, she said. *I'm liable to get arrested and shot, aren't I?*

The guard grunted and unlocked the gate and let her out. When she was a safe distance away, she couldn't help but laugh. That night, she hunkered down on the front porch of an empty farmhouse. Cattle were grazing in the field nearby, but there was not a soul in sight. She pulled out her notebook.

"I could hardly wait until I got away to burst into laughter at the ridiculous situation I had gotten into," she wrote. "The looks on those boys' faces."

6

OUR FIGHT

Her feet were a sight.

Start with the toes, which were chipped and battered and appeared almost as though she had been kicking rocks. The middle three on each foot hooked permanently downward, almost vertical from the second joint to the tip, from being scrunched into too-small shoes for too long a time. Her small toes deviated toward the center, and on the outside of both feet were large bunions.

The most astonishing thing about her feet, though, were her big toes, which jutted toward the center at a forty-five-degree angle from her instep. Protruding from the spot where the metatarsal meets the phalange on her insteps were bulbous bunions the size of ball bearings.

Her feet themselves were wide and flat and covered with veins like the lines on a map, and they ran shapelessly into oversized ankles, then up to narrow, battered, hourglass-curved shins and toward grotesque, gibbous knees surrounded by unnatural, tumorous outthrusts.

Hers were well-worn legs and she hid her feet inside sneakers and her knees inside dungarees, both of which were getting wetter by the minute. She made her way along the rugged trail in a late-June downpour, over the Priest, elevation 4,063 feet, one of the highest gains in Virginia. She tramped down across the foaming cascades of the Tye River, and on to Reeds Gap, where she lost her rain hat. She walked back a piece to find it but had no luck. She was soaked to the bone by the time she found a man milking a cow beside the trail. His name was Campbell and she asked about a place to stay. He invited her back to his house, which was way down over a hill from the trail. The woman of the house, Sis Campbell, was in her eighties, and the house looked much older than her, and its furnishings seemed to have been original. Sis Campbell led Emma upstairs by candlelight, as the old home had no electricity.

The next morning was beautiful and she walked north through central Virginia. Some passersby mentioned a restaurant, a Howard Johnson's, in the vicinity of Waynesboro to the north, and she spent much of the day's hike thinking about hot food. She stopped at the first house to ask for directions. The family, Mr. and Mrs. E. B. Ricks, were very nice and invited her in to rest. Their home was lovely. They had a flagstone courtyard and the prettiest view of the valley Emma could imagine. They were taken by her stories and asked Emma to stay for supper. Mrs. Ricks in particular wouldn't stop with the questions. After Emma went to bed, she phoned the *News Virginian* of Waynesboro.

The next morning, they drove Emma the few miles into town. She had breakfast at a restaurant, then went to the drugstore for a few items, then headed across the street and waited for another store to open so she could buy a new pair of slacks, a raincoat, and some new shoes. She had just started to shop when a man saw her and hurried toward her, grinning ear to ear.

I'm from the newspaper, he said.

They'd found her again. The reporter had phoned Mrs. Ricks and she told him that Emma was in the store shopping for shoes. Emma didn't mind so much this time. Word was out, after all. She answered all the man's questions.

Emma told him about her pack, how she had made it herself. He held it and figured it weighed about twelve pounds when full. He asked her how she had stayed warm on cold nights with no sleeping bag. She told him about heating flat rocks over a fire and reclining on them for warmth. She told him she couldn't sleep many nights for fear of bears. She hadn't seen one yet, but she'd seen plenty of signs they were around. She told him about the rattlesnake and that there weren't enough shelters along the trail and that she thought she'd finish by late September, "depending on how well I get along."

She told him about the trail magic, and how welcoming some folks had been. "I have found a lot of lovely people who have taken me in for a night's lodging and food," she said. "I have also found some who didn't care to have me around."

He asked her impressions so far, and she couldn't help herself. That *National Geographic* article made the journey seem so easy. "I have found the hike more rugged than I had heard," she said.

When the interview was over, she bought a raincoat, shoes, socks, and some food and headed off again toward the trail, then toward Sawmill Shelter. That afternoon, the story ran on the front page of the *News Virginian*, beneath the fold, under the headline: WOMAN, 67, HIKING FROM GEORGIA TO MAINE, ARRIVES IN WAYNESBORO.

Many persons take to the easy chair when they reach the age of three score and seven years.

But this is not the case for Mrs. Emma Gatewood, of Gallipolis, Ohio.

Mrs. Gatewood, the mother of 11 children whose ages range from 27 to 47, on May 3 began to hike the [2,050] mile long Appalachian Trail from Georgia to Maine.

Since May 3, the 67-year-old woman has hiked 900 miles.

The reporter asked Emma if she'd like for him to mail a clipping of his piece to her family in Ohio, three hundred miles due west of the spot where she was standing.

"The folks at home," she said, "don't know where I am."

– – – – – –

She could hide in the woods. Always.

"I've always done a lot of walking in the woods," she'd tell a newspaper reporter years later. "The stillness and quiet of the forests has always seemed so wonderful and I like the peacefulness."

Some people thought she was crazy, but she found a certain restfulness that satisfied her nature. The woods made her feel more contented. She was comfortable there, especially when her home was ruled by a tyrant. In later years, she would confide in her children that their father not only blacked her eyes and bloodied her lips but that his sexual appetite was insatiable. He demanded she submit to him several times a day. They didn't know it then, but they were used to their mother seeking haven in their beds, in the quiet of night, because she couldn't bear to lie next to him.

The children saw what he did to her, and they'd carry the memories into their old age. The muffled noises that pierced the night. The bruises on her face. The trajectory of her waning patience. Rowena, the fifth born, would always remember her mother silhouetted in an upstairs window, looking out, when a hand grabbed her hair and cast her to the floor. She would remember screaming, and her older sister slapping her face to make her stop. Louise would remember her father telling her mother she was crazy and punching her in the face with his fist. Lucy, the youngest, would remember hearing a cry and running upstairs to find her father on top of her mother, his hands around her throat, her face turning black. Nelson would remember finding his father beating his mother, and lifting his father off of her long enough for her to run away, into the woods.

They'd carry the whispers with them: That he spent his money—their money—fulfilling his desires on Two Street in Huntington, West Virginia. That he had convinced the neighbors that his wife's complaints were the complaints of an insane person. Even when he broke a broom over her head, he could convince others that he really loved her.

"Multiple times I was black and blue in a lot of places, but mostly my face," she wrote later. "I did not carry one single child that I did not get a slapping or beating during that time and several times he put me outside and told me to go. It was one grand nightmare to live with him with his maniacal temper. He would act so innocent and pretend he had not touched me and say I was not in my right mind and they would have to do something with me. He even asked me what asylum I wanted to go to and I told him Athens or O.H.E. or any place would be better than home."

She sometimes fought back, which was also part of her nature. And she could hold her own. One story would be told for years to come.

Emma and P.C. were fighting, and the farmhands were working outside. She bolted out of the house and ran around behind a wagon full of corn and scrambled up onto the produce. P.C. came out right behind her, with purpose, and he grabbed a hoe that was leaning against the house. One of the hands stopped him.

"You're gonna kill her," he said.

"Let him alone," Emma shouted. *"This is our fight."*

As their relationship deteriorated, their financial difficulties were multiplying. P.C. wrote to his well-heeled cousin, Maybelle McIntyre, in 1935, asking for a loan to save the farm, but she would not lend him money. "Can't the farm board which has such things in hand do something about it?" she wrote. P.C. shared pieces of his domestic troubles with his cousin, who lived in New York and was married to O. O. McIntyre, one of the most famous writers of the time, whose "New York Day by Day" columns ran in some five hundred newspapers. Maybelle hired P.C. in 1937 to renovate her home in Gallipolis, and when he went over the budget she had outlined, he blamed the conflicts at home.

"Naturally you must know I am very sympathetic with your domestic troubles," Maybelle responded in November 1937, "but sorry as I am it just must not enter into this business deal. If you are too troubled to get down to the reports, some one must get them to me. That is business nothing else." Three weeks later, he had paid the bills and made amends. "I feel sure if you had not had your troubles at home you would have made the reports as you went along and there would have been no worry on either side," Maybelle wrote. "However I am glad it is over and I hope your affairs there will soon clear up."

They did not clear up.

Through it all, the woods were Emma's respite. Sometimes she'd walk away and be gone all day, or long enough, at least, for his mood to shift. The forest inspired her. She wrote poetry about springtime, about the rills frolicking and zephyrs gently swaying, about the bloodroot and windflower and the hepaticas deep within the forest. She wrote of the Ohio River bends and a romantic tugboat landing. She wrote of Christmastime, and of being alone. Some of her poetry was dark and seemed to speak to how she was feeling about her relationship.

> She got her man, she has him roped
> His tongue hangs out as though he's choked
> She's sorta scared, her hair's a wreck
> She has her foot right on his neck
> Dames get desperate in times like these
> When men are scarce and hard to please

This was her lot, and she could manage, until she felt she could not. He had been so cruel she didn't know whether she'd survive another beating. As the winter of 1937 set in, she told the children who were still living at home that she loved them and would send for them. She gave the older children instructions to take care of the younger ones, and she told them to always look out for each other. And then she slipped away.

— — — — — —

The trail through the beautiful Shenandoah National Park in Virginia was good, its long, gentle ascents not nearly as taxing as the previous thousand miles of mountains. The weather was even better. She put in twenty-one miles on June 28, and twenty on June 29, fueled primarily by wild black raspberries, and on June 30, after a good morning hike and a lunch at the Big Meadows Lodge, she bumped into a Boy Scout troop at a nearby campground. When the boys learned where she had been and what she was doing they wanted her picture and autograph and she obliged. She felt a little like a celebrity.

She found shelter on Hawksbill Mountain and caught some sleep, despite the black flies that pestered her through the night.

She started at 5:30 AM the next day and was making good time through the narrow, one-hundred-mile-long park. The trail often ran alongside old stone field walls and Emma pictured someone riding in a carriage behind four horses.

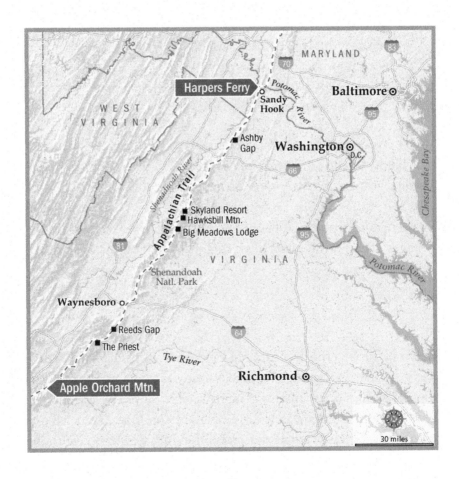

These hills had been home to Native Americans for thousands of years before European settlers began encroaching from the east, which started soon after an expedition crossed the Blue Ridge Mountains in the early 1700s. Many of the settlers came from Pennsylvania and staked out farms in the lowlands, and as prime property grew scarce they moved up into the mountains, clearing the land, hunting and trapping game and raising livestock. They made a life for themselves there for hundreds of years until the 1920s, when academics began to explore the social "problems" of the region: illiteracy, poverty, illegitimacy, sanitation.

Grand plans were launched to move the people off the mountains, pave the ridge, and transform the land into something tourists from eastern cities might enjoy riding through. In 1926 Congress authorized the establishment of Shenandoah National Park and the state began acquiring land, at times forcing people to move against their will. In 1936, President Franklin D. Roosevelt's Civilian Conservation Corps began building stone bridges, shelters, and lodges, and their handiwork was something to behold. The park was opened that year, and what once were pastures soon blossomed with the makings of what would become a mature wilderness.

Emma laid eyes on Skyland, a mountain resort opened in the 1890s by a gregarious businessman with a showman's flair, who invited city dwellers to get away from their urbanized, mechanized lives. The private resort had since been taken over by the park, but its lodges, which seemed to her to be made of bark, remained open to guests. She trudged on toward Maryland at a good clip, and on July 4, not far from Ashby Gap, she found three dollars beside the road. It was getting dark, so she used the lucky bills to get a room at a motel and ate five pieces of fried chicken—a feast.

She crossed, finally, into Maryland, into a tiny town called Sandy Hook, which was just a smattering of houses alongside the railroad tracks, not far from the Chesapeake and Ohio Canal. She introduced herself to Anna Fleming, who invited Emma to stay the night. That evening around dusk, she hiked up to Maryland Heights and sat on a cliff looking down upon the picturesque little town of Harpers Ferry, West Virginia. One hundred seventy years before, Thomas Jefferson called the view "one of the most stupendous scenes in nature." In a book first published in France, he wrote that the scene alone, the passage of the Potomac River through the Blue Ridge and its crashing merger with the Shenandoah, was worth a trip across the Atlantic.

The town below her breathed history, from the narrow brick streets and proud little buildings to the church spires and hilltop cemetery. It was the place the abolitionist John Brown believed he could spark a revolution, to turn the tide of slavery in the South and redeem an oppressed people down the barrel of a Sharps carbine. The state of Virginia hanged him for treason. His raid, though, was a catalyst for the Civil War, during which Harpers Ferry changed hands eight times in battles, the last of which came ninety-one years to the day before Emma sat upon her cliff. It was, as both sides knew, a portal to invasion. And later still, it was the place where W. E. B. Du Bois and his peers launched the Niagara Movement, which would become the National Association for the Advancement of Colored People.

So much change and inhumanity for one little place. So much bloodshed and cleansing, death and rebirth.

"The scene was beautiful," she wrote in her journal. Then, on the day after Independence Day, she stood to her feet and walked back down the trail.

7

LADY TRAMP

She could not find the trail.

Someone had told her it ran through Harpers Ferry, so she followed a road out of Sandy Hook, Maryland, and crossed the Potomac River on a railroad bridge into town. She saw old trail blazes on telephone poles near St. Peter's Roman Catholic Church, but no trail. She hiked up to a cliff looking for signs until evening, when she came back into Sandy Hook. A man there told her the trail had been rerouted, and she set off in the other direction, along the Chesapeake and Ohio Canal, making it to Weverton, just two miles away, by nightfall.

She hiked through Washington Monument State Park the next day, where the first monument to George Washington was built in 1827, and where, in the evening, she met a fire warden who invited her to sleep on a cot in his living room. He called the newspaper in Boonsboro and put Emma on the phone and here she sat, for the third time in seventeen days, answering questions she never intended to answer. It wasn't that they bothered her, but she didn't fully comprehend what the fuss was about.

The next day, as she tramped through Pen Mar Park and toward the Mason-Dixon Line, a brief dispatch from the AP was rolling off newspaper presses and being banded and loaded into bags and milk crates and onto the bicycles of boys and girls who would sling them onto the lawns and porches of hundreds of thousands of homes across the country. And as Emma hunkered down that night in a lean-to, Americans far and wide were reading the details of the long, lonely, improbable walk of a complete stranger.

BOONSBORO, MD., JULY 8 – (AP) – After 66 days and nearly 1000 miles, Mrs. Emma Gatewood is still pretty determined to become the first woman ever to hike the 2050-mile Appalachian Trail alone—even if she is 67.

The Gallipolis, Ohio, mother of 11 and grandmother of 23 emphasized this yesterday as she paused at the nearby Washington Monument State Park. At the rate she's going, Grandma Emma should make it to Mt. Katahdin, Me., sometime in September. She left the Mt. Oglethorpe, Ga., starting point, May 3.

Lugging a pack of about 35 pounds and spending the nights in her sleeping bag or some of the lean-to shelters along the way, she has worn out two pairs of shoes but none of her enthusiasm.

"I'm a great lover of the outdoors," she explained.

They got most of it right. The pack was lighter than thirty-five pounds, and she wasn't carrying a sleeping bag. And the way the hike was going, she'd be lucky to make it to Mount Katahdin by September, if she made it at all. The hardest part of the trail was ahead of her. Her celebrity was rising. More and more folks wanted her to stop and chat. Not to mention the unpredictable weather.

In the Northwest, the summer of 1955 was shaping up to be the coldest and soggiest in years. Hay was mildewing in fields and strawberries had been stunted. But Chicago was on pace to have the hottest July on record since 1871, the year before the Great Fire. Drought plagued much of the Northeast. New York had put in an appeal to the federal government for drought aid. Meanwhile, Texas was so wet the farmers had stopped talking of pulling out of the Dust Bowl. Stranger still was a rare winter storm, which had formed on New Year's Eve and developed into Hurricane Alice on January 1 before dissipating a few days later. Historians in Puerto Rico had argued about whether it was the first winter storm of its kind. They remembered a similar storm in 1816 but couldn't decide whether it had formed in September or January. Either way, the storm had meteorologists baffled. "Possibly this may be another consequence of the general warming observed during the past several decades," wrote one National Weather Bureau meteorologist.

By the end of the year, the Weather Bureau would chart thirteen tropical storms, and would note that ten of those attained hurricane force, a number that had been exceeded only once before. They'd call the hurricane season of '55 the "most disastrous in history," and note that it "broke all previous records for damage." They'd hypothesize that in July, as Emma Gatewood hiked north through Maryland unaware, a planetary wave had formed over the North Atlantic and evolved like a tropical storm, and that at the ridge of the Azores, upper level anticyclone circulation thrust strongly northeastward into Europe and introduced a northeasterly flow that, through vorticity flux, produced an anomalously sharp and deep trough extending along the Spanish and African coasts.

And at the base of that trough, they'd write, its genesis encouraged by the injection of cyclonic vorticity from the north and associated vertical destabilization, another storm would be born.

Emma Gatewood knew none of this. Her world was insular, the trees and flowers and animals and elements. She drifted to sleep that night in a lean-to beside the trail.

The boys came, three of them, around midnight to camp at the shelter, and when they discovered an old woman inside, they turned to leave. Emma invited them back, told them there was plenty of room and she didn't mind at all to share the space. She left them

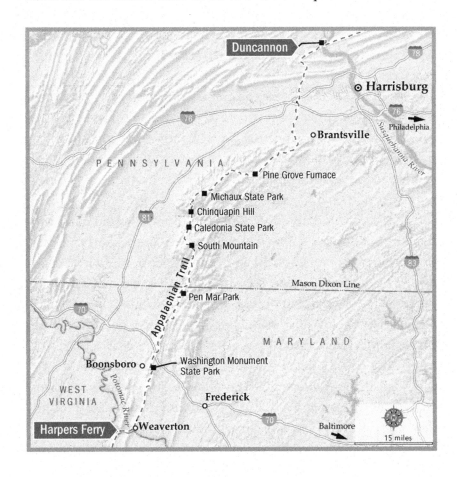

sleeping the next morning and made good time across the state line into Pennsylvania, nearing Caledonia State Park, in a valley between Blue Mountain and South Mountain, land once owned by Thaddeus Stevens. She'd be in Pennsylvania for another 230 miles. She washed out some clothes and dried them by a fire and slept some before setting off again.

She was climbing up the steep south bank of Chinquapin Hill when she heard something unnatural. She swung around and caught sight of a man who was huffing and puffing up the slope behind her. His hair fell in his eyes and he was having a hard time with the climb, but it seemed he wanted to catch up. Figuring he was a reporter, she stopped.

The man introduced himself as Warren Large. He was a birdwatcher, and he'd read about her in the newspaper and set out that morning to try to find her. He said that he wouldn't take too much of her time, he just wanted to ask a few questions. Two or three, he said. The two sat on a log in the Pennsylvania woods and started talking. Two hours later, he said he'd better go. He got up and bid Emma good-bye and lots of luck. Then he sat back down and they went on talking another hour. On July 10, 1955, Warren Large missed church and Sunday school and Emma Gatewood called it a day.

She got a nice bunch of lettuce from Mrs. Meisenhalter in Michaux and some provisions in Pine Grove Furnace, finally arriving at the halfway point on the trail, a place named for its charcoal-fired blast furnace where firearms were made for the American Revolution. She was talking to the leader of a Boy Scout pack from Ohio when the forest warden called her to the telephone. It was the state park superintendent. He wanted to arrange an appointment with Conway Robinson, a radio and newspaper reporter from Baltimore. News had finally hit the big cities. Robinson wanted to meet Emma in Brantsville, Pennsylvania, so the next morning she started early, before 6:00 AM, but she got lost on a side trail. By the time she found her way, it was inching into afternoon and she still had miles to go. The section was particularly rocky, and everywhere she turned there were more rocks. It was 5:00 PM by the time she arrived in Brantsville. Robinson had been waiting all afternoon, but he took her back to the woods before sundown and shot photographs and film of her walking around. When he had enough, he recorded her voice. As a way of saying thanks, Robinson treated her to supper that evening.

— — — — — —

She walked across the Pacific Coast Highway and into the sand and across the beach of an ocean she had never before seen. She wore Sunday shoes and a long-sleeved linen dress and a straw sun hat with a white flower affixed to the side. The California wind blew the saltwater and sand against her skin. A group of boys in full-length bathing suits splashed in the surf. The year was 1937.

She stared at the ocean and beheld its simple beauty. So far from home, she wondered about her daughters.

She had slipped away to come west, a journey most of her family had made years before. Her mother and a brother were in California, and a sister had a place in Santa Ana—and an extra bed. She had relayed that it would be no bother to have a houseguest until things settled down in Gallia County. Emma enjoyed catching up, and her mother offered warm sympathies for her struggles back home. But the sadness of leaving her children had left Emma heartbroken. She couldn't have afforded to make it here with them, and she knew that P.C. wouldn't treat them like he had treated her. She'd moved to California once before, bringing Louise, an infant, after a brutal beating, but it was temporary. She

First sight of ocean, between Seal and Huntington Beaches, 1926.
Courtesy Lucy Gatewood Seeds

stayed for nearly a year, then moved back to Ohio when P.C. promised things would change. This time was different. She wasn't sure
she'd ever go back.

Emma felt pangs of guilt for leaving her children. But what
choice did she have? P.C. had violated her for the last time, and if
she wasn't strong enough to keep him away, her only option was to
leave, to head west.

On November 18, 1937, she wrote to her daughters and tucked
the two-page letter into an envelope with no return address.

Dear Louise and Lucy:

I have wanted to write to you all the time but did not want your dad to know where I was. He is the worst nightmare I ever heard of. I wish to the great I am he would leave me alone. I do not want him around and he just might as well give up. Yesterday he wired me a large bunch of mums and not wanting to look at them I immediately took them to the cemetery and put them on Father's and Myrta's graves. I will bet you could use a new dress, shoes, or coat. I can not possibly ever think of coming back while he is there and there is not any use for him to keep pestering me. I try not to think of you and all the things I could and would love to do for you. Will just live in hopes things will change so that I can be with you sometime. You be patient and good so that you will not cause so much misery as your dad has. I would still be with you if he had just kept his hand to himself in spite of all the ugly things he said to me. But that is all past now. It is just too bad and too late. If he bothers me anymore I will go to some foreign country and I will bet he will not bother me. I hope I will never see his old face again. I have suffered enough at his hands to last me for the next hundred years.

Living in hopes I can be with you again sometime, I am yours with tons of love,

Mama

The girls read the letter at home in Gallia County. They were eleven and nine and old enough to understand the pain packed into it. They had been their father's tools, too, writing at his command about how much they missed her and how much they wanted to see her and how she should, please, come home. They knew, even then, that they were part of a charade, but they cooperated. And the letters continued.

— — — — — —

The road was flat and barren, a two-lane ribbon of asphalt that unspooled before her, and she thought it would never end. Her feet were sore. All day she was on the highway, and she hiked over the new Pennsylvania Turnpike, America's first toll road, which extended east to the Delaware River and west to her home state of Ohio. She saw a house around 5:30 that evening, and without even asking, she walked up and plopped down on the front porch. The people inside, the McAllister family, looked through the windows at the scruffy stranger. She got the impression that they thought she was batty, and she wasn't about to correct them. She was too tired. They finally asked her who she was and Emma told them what she was doing. They warmed up a bit and invited her to supper, and once they had eaten, the McAllisters asked if she wanted to stay the night.

The next day the hike took her over sharp, jagged rocks all morning, remnants of the glaciers of the last ice age that scraped them south before retreating. The section was the rockiest on the trail, and each stone seemed to be purposefully placed on edge. She desperately needed new shoes. She had sliced the sides of the pair she was wearing to make them more comfortable, to give her bunions room to breathe, but her feet were swelling from all the walking.

A little after 11:00, she arrived on the outskirts of Duncannon, Pennsylvania. She was wearing Bermuda shorts and she was already in town by the time she thought about changing into her dungarees. A cluster of children were playing on their front porch and, upon seeing her coming up the road, one little boy hollered.

"Look!" he told his playmates. "There goes a lady tramp!"

Emma kept walking. It wasn't the first or last time she'd been pointed out in derision, and she didn't let it stop her. A few minutes later, the lady tramp crossed the mighty Susquehanna River and popped into a little restaurant at the end of the bridge. She ordered a tomato sandwich and chased it with a banana split to lift her spirits.

After her dinner, she went in search of water. By 9:00 PM, she still hadn't found any. She fished her flashlight from her sack and stood beside the road, waving the light in hopes a car would stop. When one finally did, it held two women and their children. Emma told them she was looking for a place to stay—or some water at least. She piled in and they drove fifteen miles before the woman pulled up to a house where Emma spent the night. The homeowner drove her back to the trail the next morning.

Besides the throbbing in her feet, the hike through eastern Pennsylvania, about one hundred miles west of Philadelphia then, was easy. The difficulty was finding a place to stay. She walked fifteen miles on July 15 before she approached a large house to ask if they had extra room. She could see a woman inside doing housework, but when the woman came to the door she claimed she had arthritis and wouldn't invite Emma in. At the next house she came to, the homeowner said he didn't have any extra beds or room. She tried eight houses in a row and was turned away at each one.

The next house she came to was little bitty, and a buxom blonde answered the door. The woman said she didn't have an extra bed, but she sent the children to an outbuilding, where they prepared a cot for Emma. She told them she preferred the front porch swing, if that was OK, and she fell asleep there that hot summer night as the woman washed her clothes in a machine.

8

ATTENTION

The sharp rocks were killing her feet, each step a new jolt of pain. Emma didn't wear the hard-soled boots of a seasoned outdoorsman but rubber-soled sneakers that quickly wore out. In an emergency, she had taped the discarded rubber heel from a man's shoe to the bottom of her instep for more arch support. Her footwear was more akin to the moccasins worn by Daniel Boone, who was born in the vicinity and used to hunt and fish in these hills as a boy.

Happy to let her feet heal, she spent the night at the Hertlein Campsite and made it into the narrow little town of Port Clinton, Pennsylvania, the next afternoon. She poked into a store to see about getting a new pair of shoes. The place was a wreck, the worst disorder she'd ever seen. Boxes were piled high and there was a layer of dust on everything she touched. She bought a few snacks and sat on the porch out front for a bit before heading down the street to see about a room at the King Fish Hotel. Just then, a woman in a nearby house hollered.

Are you the woman who is walking the trail? she asked.

I am, said Emma.

The woman, Mrs. Swayberger, was very excited, and that made Emma happy. The woman told her son to stand next to Emma for a photograph, and the woman's daughter insisted Emma follow her around the corner to meet her husband, who was interested in the trail.

She had again been recognized. Word about her hike was spreading like prairie fire. The Associated Press dispatch from Boonsboro, Maryland, had made it all the way to Gallia County, in fact, and the newspaper ran a follow-up story on the local woman who was getting national attention.

Her exact whereabouts since she left here early in April to "go south" were not known until Friday afternoon when word came from Boonsboro, Md., of her progress along the trail which winds from Mt. Oglethorpe, Ga., through 14 states, eight national forests and two national parks, to its northern terminus atop Mt. Katahdin, Maine, some 5,200 feet above sea level.

The reporter interviewed Monroe, Emma's oldest son, who was the wire chief for Ohio Bell Telephone Company in Gallia County. Monroe seemed surprised, but not worried.

"We did not know for sure what she was doing until just yesterday, although we were beginning to have our suspicions," he said. "Mother is a great lover of the outdoors, enjoys perfect health, and can outwalk most persons many years younger."

On a stretch of the A.T. through Berks County, Pennsylvania, Emma bumped into a group of Boy Scouts from the Shikellamy Scout Reservation, who promptly reported back to a columnist at the *Reading Eagle*. Emma had told the boys that she'd so far detoured for three copperheads and two rattlesnakes, and that she'd slept outdoors on a handful of freezing nights. The boys were mystified that she was wearing tennis shoes, the columnist reported. "She was wearing sneakers, and supposedly expert counsel on hiking comfort advises the wearing of stout shoes of good weight—not too heavy but tough enough to stand hard wear," the columnist wrote. "When you're a 67-year-old woman on a 2,050-mile hike, though, maybe there isn't another person in the world who qualifies as an expert on how to take care of your own feet."

News of her walk had even reached a young writer at a fledgling magazine called *Sports Illustrated* in New York City. Reporter Mary Snow began to wonder whether the eccentric grandmother on the Appalachian Trail might make for a good profile. The newspaper stories had addressed the *Who, What, Where, When,* and *How,* but no reporter had touched on the most important, intriguing question: *Why?* Snow would. But first things first: how do you track down someone in the wilderness who is hiking at a clip of fourteen miles a day?

Meanwhile, Emma had her own problems, besides her swollen feet. She had left Port Clinton, Pennsylvania, after a good night's rest, enjoyed a lovely walk the next afternoon, bunked in a cabin at Blue Mountain for a dollar, then headed for Palmerton, Pennsylvania, on the morning of July 19. She tried to rent a hotel room, but the folks there wouldn't let her stay. She wondered what she must look like. She had found a faucet that morning and washed her face, but without a comb she had no way to brush the knots out of her iron-gray hair. She had sifted through a campfire and found a fork, which she used as a comb. Now, though, she was leaving yet another hotel, exhausted and wondering where she should go for the night.

She was walking down the road's shoulder when a car pulled up beside her in the dusk. Driving was a young woman from the hotel who appeared burdened by her conscience. She asked Emma to climb in, saying she wanted to take her into Palmerton proper. A few minutes later they pulled up at a hotel and Emma got a room for the night for two dollars. She soaked her feet in a bath and walked down the street to Sally's Restaurant for a sandwich. Someone there told her she needed to meet Ralph Leh and the waitress, Sally, got him on the phone.

Leh, bespectacled and seventy, was retired from New Jersey Zinc Co., and he was quite the hiker himself. Besides climbing Mount Washington, he had spent the spring before helping clear the Appalachian Trail to Devil's Pulpit on the Lehigh Gap. He knew that section of the trail like the back of his hand.

Leh invited Emma to stay at his house, so she fetched her bag from the hotel and showed up on his front porch. The two talked into the night, forming a bond that would last for years. Leh called up the newspaper in Allentown and two journalists came for yet another interview. The reporter asked her what surprised her most about the hike.

"All the publicity the newspapers give me," she said.

The next morning, Leh drove her across town to a store called Grant's, which wasn't yet open for the day. Once Leh explained who his company was, the clerk obliged and invited them in, pleased to accommodate. Emma scanned the aisle for a pair of women's shoes that would fit, but the largest size was much too small. Her feet had swollen out of women's shoes. She slipped into a comfortable pair of men's shoes, size 8½, which gave her a little room should her feet continue to expand. She bought the shoes, two pairs of wool and nylon socks, and some wire hairpins. The clerk, out of kindness, gave her three five-cent packages of Life Savers and wished her lots of luck.

Leh drove Emma back to Lehigh Gap, where she had left the trail, and the two climbed the cliff to the top. Leh thought Emma might need help getting up the steep embankment, but he was surprised to see her scale the wall, lugging her bag and maple walking stick, without help.

He bid her good-bye from below and, again, she was alone.

— — — — —

Emma wrote to her daughters again on February 20, 1938, from her sister Lucy's house in Santa Ana, California, where she had found a job working as a practical nurse. She was burdened deeply by her decision to leave her family and peeved by the repeated attempts from her husband to lure her home. Nevertheless, she was considering returning, even then.

Dear Louise and Lucy:

It is dear of you to write to me and send the nice candy and valentines. I like the pictures you draw and am so glad you are getting along so nicely in school. I hope I can be with you sometime and do all the nice little things I would love to do. . . . I have a lovely place to stay and there is loads of lovely flowers of all kinds. I would tell you more only your dad would write to the man in the mountains with lots of flowers and such and such a house etc. etc. like he did when I was at Orange. I have Sunday off and spend it here with Mother. It is quite a little drive but it is nice to be with Mother. Don't you think it would be nice to be with your mother? I picked some oranges and made some fruit salad for dinner or lunch as the city folks say. . . . My side hurts pretty badly sometimes. Some nights I can hardly get to sleep for the pain. I want to have it seen to as soon as I can. It should make your Dad feel good to know he did it, throwing me down in the floor. My breast is still blue where he jumped on me, but the lump is gone. I go to bed now and everything is just as peaceful and quiet as can be. Hoping you are fine and be nice girls so I can be proud of you.

With loads of love,

Mama

The pain in her side was getting worse, and though she was working six days a week, she couldn't easily afford to see a doctor. In the days after she mailed the letter, she devised a plan. She'd return home to be with her daughters and P.C. would have to pay for her medical care, whatever that might entail.

The decision would almost kill her.

— — — — — —

The Delaware Water Gap, with its scenic overlooks and rhododendron tunnels and magnificent waterfalls, was just ahead, and she was walking hard to get there before dark. She was coming down out of an upthrust of rocks on Kittatinny Mountain, in a hurry to find a place to stay before night set in, when she slipped.

The fall wasn't bad, but she felt a short, sharp pain in her knee. She examined the injury and tested the knee under her full weight. To her relief, the sprain wasn't severe, but even a minor injury on the trail can be devastating, especially when it's exacerbated by continuous pounding. Ahead were the toughest, tallest mountains, in New Hampshire and Vermont and Maine, and she'd need to be in

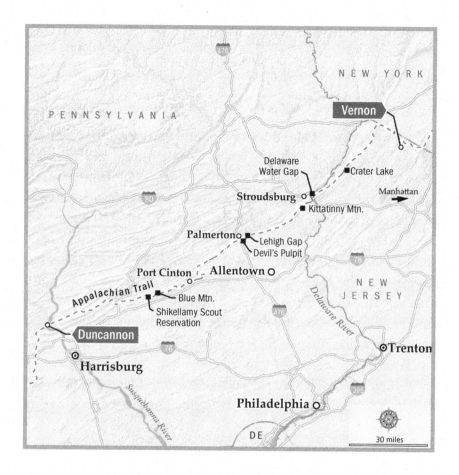

top condition. She walked on and found a pool of water and some picnic tables in the dark. Someone had told her there weren't any houses in the vicinity, so she made her bed on one of the tables and tried to find sleep.

She didn't know whether she had made her bed at the local make-out spot or what, but at several times during the night, headlights would swing across the bend as cars pulled into the park. And every time, upon catching sight of the worn-out human sprawled on the picnic table, the cars spun around and sped away, as if something were chasing them, leaving behind an old woman, half asleep and chuckling.

— — — — — —

She wasn't on the trail but five minutes the morning of July 22 when she came to a village—so near to where she'd had a terrible time trying to sleep. Hotels, motels, restaurants, houses. The time was 5:45 AM, so nothing was open, but she waited around a bit, hoping to grab a bite to eat before she set off again. A couple men noticed her on the sidewalk and told her the restaurants didn't open until 8:00 AM. She couldn't wait that long, so she set off across the bridge over the Delaware River and into New Jersey, the eighth state she'd walked through in eighty days. She hadn't made it far into New Jersey when a Jeep pulled up beside her and the driver rolled down his window. He was wearing a police uniform.

What's your name? the man asked.

Emma wondered what she had done wrong. She thought, by the way he had said it, that she was in trouble. Maybe he mistook her for a vagrant.

Emma Gatewood, she said.

You're wanted on the telephone, the man said. He opened the door on the passenger side, and she climbed in and they drove to his office not far away. A *Sports Illustrated* reporter named Mary Snow wanted Emma to call her collect in New York City. It took her an hour to get through and the officer poured Emma a glass of milk and gave her a doughnut while she dialed. When she finally reached Mary Snow, the two chatted for a while and Snow asked Emma to call her on Monday to let Snow know her location. She asked if she could tag along for a bit and write a profile of the hiking grandmother. Emma didn't see a problem with that. She promised to call.

The next day was a bitter disappointment. The trail was difficult, high above the Delaware River Valley on Kittatinny Ridge, and she did not make it far on her sprained knee. She slept beside the path, three miles from Crater Lake. A deer came in the night, snorting, and she was glad it wasn't a bear. She stayed the next night in the High Point Monument, an obelisk built to honor the war dead, and the next in a rest home, of all places, where she had plopped down on the grass out front and waited for the proprietor to invite her in.

On July 26, she made it to the Appalachian Lodge in Vernon, New Jersey, and found a bed in a shed on an army cot. If she kept the pace, by the next afternoon she'd be in New York, nearing the Hudson River Valley, where she was to meet Mary Snow.

9

GOOD HARD LIFE

JULY 27–AUGUST 2, 1955

Just south of the hardscrabble river city of Port Jervis, New York, she turned south and snaked along the state line, the low and fertile black-dirt region to her east, until the trail turned north near Greenwood Lake, New York, then back to the east, toward the Palisades Interstate Park, forty miles north of Manhattan and the millions of people rushing about in the city.

At Lake Mombasha, she met a man and two children who were going for a swim. The man said the lake was private property before starting up the trail. Emma followed them, talking about the trail and chattering about her walk until the man grew interested. She pulled from her bag a few of the newspaper clippings she had collected and was showing the man when a woman walked up and introduced herself as Mary Snow.

Emma wasn't able to reach her on Monday or Tuesday when she called, so she was surprised to see Snow waiting. They chatted a while and made plans to meet a few hours later where the trail crossed Route 17, which carried white-knuckled tourists from the city to the Catskill Mountains and back. Snow then said good-bye. Emma started walking and came to a steep and dangerous rock scramble surging skyward called Agony Grind, known to make grown men say embarrassing things. Emma, on a bum leg, would later write in her diary that it was a "pretty hard and rocky piece of trail."

When she reached Route 17, Snow was waiting with a police officer's wife. They drove together to the officer's house for lunch, then back to the trail, where Emma and her new acquaintance started walking. They talked along the way, with Snow asking question after question. Emma told her she'd carefully avoided snakes and other critters. She talked about eating plants and berries, sustenance she found along the trail, and about relying on the charity of strangers. She mentioned that she'd met both nice and miserable people. She seemed serenely confident that she'd make it to Maine.

She told Snow something else. When she stood on top of Mount Katahdin—*if* she made it to the top of Mount Katahdin—she planned to do something special.

The trail was smooth and easy, and after five miles they reached a new stone shelter on Fingerboard Mountain. Snow told Emma she'd meet her the next morning at 9:30 on Bear Mountain, a few miles away, hard against the Hudson River. There were two boys at the shelter, which was built atop a huge boulder. It had a tin roof and fireplaces at both ends, and it was filthy.

Emma decided to sleep outside instead, and she found a nice grassy spot on which to spread her blanket. The boys moved down behind a large rock, in some leaves. Emma felt raindrops in the night, so she grabbed her bag and scrambled through the dark to the shelter. She turned her flashlight on for the boys, who seemed content to sleep in the rain. She needed rest, though. She had to be up early to make it to Bear Mountain on time. And the climb ahead would be rough.

— — — — — —

Emma returned from California to a financial mess. P.C. had mismanaged the farm in her absence. They had no money to pay the mortgage and could not find a way to appease the creditors. In 1938, they had to let the farm go.

They bought the smaller George Sheets farm up the river from Crown City, Ohio, and moved in on May 30, but they would be gone by the following year. Something had gotten into P.C. He would not let Emma out of his sight. He refused to work unless she came along, whether it was building fences or pounding rock or cutting wood.

Occasionally, Emma would slip a few sandwiches into a paper bag and take her two young daughters into the woods to hunt for wildflowers. They'd walk over hills and into valleys all day long, identifying bloodroot and windflowers, bluets and buttercups and trilliums. On one of their flower hunts near Possum Hollow, a gentle rain was falling, washing the woodlands, and they found a large, moss-covered boulder protruding from the earth, covered with delicate hepaticas. It was a sight they'd never forget.

Emma would later write that her husband beat her beyond recognition ten times that year.

— — — — — —

The reporters gathered early near the observatory on Bear Mountain on July 28, a bevy of them with Mary Snow of *Sports Illustrated*, to wait for Grandma Emma Gatewood, who would be arriving at 9:30 AM. Ten o'clock passed, then eleven, then noon, and there was no sign yet of Emma. The newspapermen and photographers began to peel away, one by one, disappointed and a bit worried about the old woman. Mary Snow held out, but ventured down the mountain for lunch.

Emma had walked as hard as she could to make it on time, but the section of trail was steep and her injury made the climb difficult. She caught up with a group of hikers, though, and asked them how far she was from Bear Mountain.

Seven miles, one of them said. They pointed to a peak on the horizon and off she went.

By the time she arrived at the top, four hours late, all of the reporters had gone. Mary Snow and a tall policeman soon arrived and the policeman took photographs of Emma, hand on her hip, a green eyeshade pulled down over her nut-brown forehead, her sack slung over her left shoulder. A few tourists noticed and began snapping her picture as well. When the policeman was finished, Emma headed down the mountain and Snow met her in a car at the bottom and took her to a restaurant. That night Snow paid for a cabin in Fort Montgomery, on the west bank of the Hudson. Emma said goodbye, then washed her clothes and dried them by a fire and fell asleep.

She had tried to find a map but had no luck, so the next morning at 6:00 AM she walked back to where Snow had fetched her and found the nearest white blaze and followed it toward the Bear Mountain Bridge, an impressive suspension bridge of steel and concrete, completed thirty-one years before. She noticed the railroad tracks running underneath the automobile lanes. She had never dreamed she would get to walk across the Hudson River on a bridge, but step-by-step she went as cars blurred by. She stopped in the middle, suspended between the water and the sky, to behold the sights. Downriver was New York City, and to the north was the

United States Military Academy at West Point, where monuments to dead soldiers dotted the manicured grounds. It was here, during the Revolutionary War, that colonists stretched a giant chain across the Hudson to stop British ships from traveling upriver.

Across the bridge, she walked over swampy but level ground and stumbled onto a Girl Scout camp about 8:00 AM. The campers were still sleeping, so Emma routed them out from their beds. They'd intended to get up early to break camp. She pressed on and slept that night on a pile of leaves near the trail.

She left again at 5:30 AM, thirsty and looking for water, and walked until she heard the gurgle of a stream. Following the sound she found a new well, but the water flowing out was muddy. She approached the house nearby and a woman kindly filled her canteen and offered Emma breakfast.

Farther down the trail, near Stormville, New York, in the Fishkill Mountains, she came to something called the Lost Village. It appeared to be a museum, so she wandered in. The Lost Village had been open just two months, and its proprietors had recently made the controversial claim that the American cowboy had originated there, a short commute from New York City, despite the legends of the West. Two city dwellers had found the place several years before, on a weekend trip upstate to look for land. They discovered several stone foundations and various pieces of pottery and iron kettles and, after reviewing some historical maps, decided to campaign publicly that the original "cowboys" were British cattle thieves who raided rich Dutch settlers from a lawless encampment on the mountain. It helped that the husband was a publicist and the wife a writer. The newspapers ran stories. The proprietors charged admission at the door.

Emma didn't dispute the claims. She looked around, then left, and jotted her feelings later in her diary. "Some things there were fakes, I am sure," she wrote.

As the sun set July 30, she followed a side trail to the Ludington Girl Scout Camp, near Holmes, New York, the village from which the first thru-hiker, Earl V. Shaffer, had mailed his groundbreaking letter to the Appalachian Trail Conference. Emma introduced herself. The counselors asked her to stay, and after dinner they parked Emma in front of the fireplace and sat the girls at her feet, little ones in the front. She told them story after story about her trip. When she was finished, all the girls wanted her autograph. In a shaky hand, Emma signed every scrap of paper.

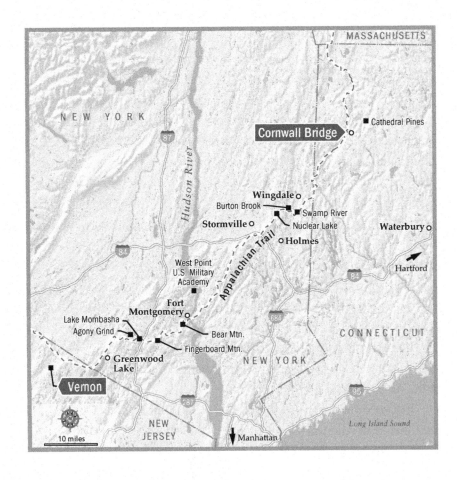

She slept on a cot in a tent that night and the kitchen staff sent her away early the next morning with a full belly, a sack lunch for the trail, and a handful of bouillon cubes. She hiked the next day past Nuclear Lake and over Burton Brook and Swamp River and made it to another Girl Scout camp in Wingdale, New York, by nightfall and again enjoyed the company, and the dinner of steamed brown bread and celery.

On the first day of August, she left New York and entered Connecticut, the ninth state in which she'd planted her sneakers. She wanted to make it twenty miles up the Housatonic River Valley to Cornwall Bridge, Connecticut, before dark, but despite walking hard all day, she hadn't reached town when the sky went black. As she was hoofing down the shoulder of a gravel mountain road, a car stopped beside her and a man with booze-hazed eyes looked her over.

Why in the world are you walking in such a place after night for? he asked.

She told him she was trying to make it to town before dark.

Get in, he said in a demanding tone. *I'll take you to my sister's a half-mile down the road.*

She hesitated. She wasn't sure she trusted him.

Get on in here, he said. *You can't get to Cornwall Bridge tonight.*

She did as he said, but she wasn't sure it was wise. His appearance was dulled, and Emma was pretty sure he was full of strong drink, but he did what he promised. The man's sister, Mrs. Charles Moore, wouldn't hear of Emma going any farther that night.

Emma woke early and walked back to where the man had picked her up, then back to the Moores' for breakfast. She'd come this far without skipping a single step of the trail, and she wasn't about to start cheating. She hiked the five miles into Cornwall Bridge and poked into the post office to see if she had any mail. She didn't. She called the home of Patrick Hare, a local man she had met at

Shenandoah National Park, but no one answered. She ate dinner at the home of Mrs. Clarence Blake, a correspondent for the local newspaper.

The story in the *Waterbury Republican* ran the next day, as Emma followed the trail along a picturesque ravine, past clear waterfalls, and under a tall hemlock canopy that excluded most of the sunlight, then through a plateau of giant boulders and into the majestic Cathedral Pines, an old-growth white-pine and hemlock forest with trees reaching more than one hundred feet into the sky.

GREAT-GRANDMOTHER GUNS ALONG, the headline read.

Blake noted that Emma had worn out three pairs of shoes and had lost twenty-four pounds in the three months she'd been walking. "Even the beginning of the hike was done on a spur of the moment basis. Mrs. Gatewood just started out equipped with a canteen, a 25-pound pack and some 'spending money,'" the article read. "Mrs. Gatewood has had no special training as a hiker, except for the good hard life of raising her 11 children on a farm in Ohio." The article spoke of her determination, and how she had established a pace of about seventeen miles per day, "rain or shine."

The shine part was easy.

10

STORM

On the morning of August 3, sailors aboard the SS *Mormacreed*, traveling off the coast of French Guiana, noticed unusually strong winds blowing in from the west. They carried showery, squally weather. Around the same time and several hundred miles north, a freighter called the *African Sun* passed through a strong easterly wave that tossed the massive ship like a doll. At 10:00 AM, another vessel, the SS *Bonaire*, radioed the National Weather Bureau in Miami, Florida, to report a falling barometric pressure and north-easterly winds blowing at more than forty miles per hour. Waves were breaking at twenty feet and it was becoming clear that a vortex had formed at the top end of the easterly wave.

A hurricane was born.

A reconnaissance plane spotted the eye of the storm, which was pushing winds at fifty-five knots and surging west-northwest over the warm North Atlantic waters at sixteen miles per hour, slowly increasing in size and intensity, sucking up moist tropical air from the surface and discharging cooler air aloft, breathing in and out and growing as if it were a living thing. When the eye of the storm passed fifty miles north of the northern Leeward Islands and Puerto Rico, maximum winds were estimated at 125 miles per hour and the storm had splayed heavy rain bands, like fingers, for miles in all directions.

In the coming days, Hurricane Connie would change direction, stall, spin north, then northwest, avoiding Florida and lining up to slam North Carolina and rake its way up the Atlantic seaboard toward southern New England, toward towns that would need new maps and people who would lose their lives and their loved ones and spend terrible hours clinging to treetops as floodgates crashed and rivers escaped their banks.

In those slow days before the hurricane made landfall, though, before the obituaries had been written and before the nation's news magazines had questioned whether the weather of 1955 was the worst in recorded history, the people of New England set about their daily routines. The same was true for the stranger in the tiny town of Amesville, Connecticut, who woke at Eva Bates's house a little before six o'clock, slung her bag on her shoulder, and rejoined the Appalachian Trail. Emma walked until she came to a low, swampy stretch in the woods, where the mosquitoes rose from the earth in thick clouds. She slapped at them a few times and then hurried to higher ground, where she stopped to thin them out.

Sick of fighting the biting bugs, she walked into a town to pick up some repellant oil from a dime store. Salisbury, Connecticut, wasn't much more than a wide spot in the road, but years before, it was known as the "Arsenal of the Revolution." For two hundred years, men pulled iron ore from the ground and shaped it into implements and guns and cannons.

As Emma was leaving town, a woman recognized her as the hiking grandmother from the newspaper and called out across the street. She invited Emma inside and served her milk and sweet cakes. A few minutes after she had started down the trail again, she saw a man standing in the road with a camera hanging around his neck. He asked her if he could take her photograph. She didn't mind. Ten minutes later, a reporter from the paper stopped her again and questioned her about the journey. This was becoming routine, and she wondered if she'd ever make it to Maine.

She surged forward, up Lions Head at the southern end of the Taconic Range, up Bear Mountain, the highest summit in Connecticut, across the Sages Ravine, its waterfalls dancing over moss-covered rock, where she saw her first porcupine, then into Massachusetts, leaving nine states behind her now on day number ninety-three.

That afternoon, she hiked a ways with a pack of Boy Scouts, but by nightfall they had not found shelter and so the boys stopped to set up camp. Emma left them behind and climbed Mount Everett. There she found a fire tower but could not find a shelter. Everett's vistas were breathtaking, but it was too rocky to sleep on the precipice, so she went a bit farther and raked together a pile of leaves beside a boulder as darkness fell.

Before she drifted off, Emma heard a voice. It belonged to one of the scout leaders. She got up and found them at the summit, flashlight beams shining through the trees, where they were searching for the shelter. Even with a trail map the leaders could not find it. They left the scouts with Emma and went stomping around in the darkness. The boys looked thirsty, and Emma had a little water in her canteen. She offered it to them, but they refused to take it. When the leaders returned, she went back to her trailside bed of leaves.

The rain started the next day, on August 5.

What was already a slow slog grew slower. Emma made it just two and a half miles in the morning. She met a man that afternoon, Joe Seifert of Newark, New Jersey, who was thru-hiking the trail in the opposite direction, from north to south. They talked an hour but the downpour grew so heavy they could not continue their conversation. After sunset, Emma noticed a cluster of three houses, but no one would invite her in. She climbed over another mountain in the rain and finally found a kind soul, a woman named Mrs. Norris. The next evening, after another day of hiking through the rain, she tried to stay with a man named Moore, but he didn't have room. He offered his car. She reclined in the seat and caught a decent night's sleep. It was better than a picnic table by a mile.

The rain clouds parted momentarily the next morning and Emma hiked into Washington, Massachusetts, where Mrs. Fred Hutchinson started to fill her canteen, thinking she was a berry picker, until Emma spoke up and got herself invited to dinner, then to a nap on the couch, then to the obligatory newspaper interview, then to a night in a bed.

— — — — — —

The morning of Monday, August 8, Emma traversed Warner Hill and Tully Mountain, near Pittsfield, Massachusetts, and was approaching Dalton when Hurricane Connie reached its maximum intensity five hundred miles east of West Palm Beach, Florida, moving north-northwest at fifteen miles per hour, drawing a bead on the East Coast. Its winds were churning at 135 miles per hour near the eye, and gales extended 350 miles farther north. A navy reconnaissance plane measured the eye. It was forty miles wide.

The pilot, Lt. Commander R. T. Pittman of Covington, Georgia, called Hurricane Connie "the biggest storm I've ever seen."

Another, Lieutenant Alfred M. Fowler of Waterloo, Iowa, gave this description:

> In the eye, you would think you were sitting in the middle of a big amphitheatre. All around you in a huge circle were bands of white clouds. Below was a deck of stratocumulus clouds and above was the bright blue sky. We flew up to 10,000 feet and the walls of the amphitheater still rose above us.

It was hot and wet in the center, as well, full of eighty-six-degree tropical air.

The National Weather Bureau issued small craft warnings for boats from Block Island, Rhode Island, to Cape Hatteras, North Carolina, as people along the Atlantic Coast brought lawn furniture inside and stocked up on nonperishables and hammered storm shutters over windows. The bureau called it a "severe" hurricane, but no one yet knew the course the storm would choose.

"We're sweating it out," Walter Davis, a storm warning forecaster in Miami, told the Associated Press. "Our best judgment is that Connie will be affected by the southern portion of the trough and will turn northward, then northeastward. Time will tell."

By that afternoon, as Emma popped into the post office at Dalton, where the clerk recognized her and introduced her to everyone in the room, the giant storm rushed northwest, swelling, gaining strength. Warning flags flapped from Cape Lookout, North Carolina, to Norfolk, Virginia, and the tides grew by three feet. Seven hundred airmen from the air force, army, navy, and marines hustled to move planes and vehicles inland from the coast, to Spartanburg, South Carolina. Giant waves lapped at coastal beaches and gales of seventy-five miles per hour stretched three hundred miles north of the eye. The North Carolina Highway Patrol, Red Cross disaster specialists, and Civil Air Patrol personnel organized for rescue missions.

That evening, as Emma walked into Cheshire, Massachusetts, and checked in at Leroy's Tourist Home, something else had become evident in the Atlantic, as well. Ships traveling five hundred miles from the northernmost Leeward Islands, well behind the hurricane, were reporting new bands of heavy rain and east winds up to forty-five miles per hour. While Hurricane Connie slogged toward the coast, another threatening storm was developing in its wake.

The second storm had forecasters baffled. Would it peter out and disappear in the Atlantic? Would it weaken as another trough passed to the north? Or would it intensify and follow Connie toward the United States, setting up a nightmarish situation for the people along the coast?

— — — — —

Before her, through the dark and low-slung clouds that raced north on the morning of August 9, stood the highest point in Massachusetts: Greylock Mountain. If the Berkshires behind her were light and inviting, Greylock, at 3,491 feet, served as a domineering challenge.

The mountain inspired some of the greatest authors of American literature. Herman Melville drew inspiration from Greylock while working on *Moby-Dick*, 105 years before Emma marched through. He thought the mountain looked like a whale, and he had a view of it from his writing room in Pittsfield. Henry David Thoreau wrote about his 1844 climb in *A Week on the Concord and Merrimack Rivers*, summiting the mountain a year before his experiment at Walden Pond. There was, no doubt, something special about the mountain, but the two men took distinctly different views. The themes in *A Week* and Melville's "The Piazza," a story set on Greylock, both involve a man on a quest who meets a woman. To the narrator in "The Piazza," the woman, a "fairy queen sitting at her fairy-window," represents a disappointment; he had

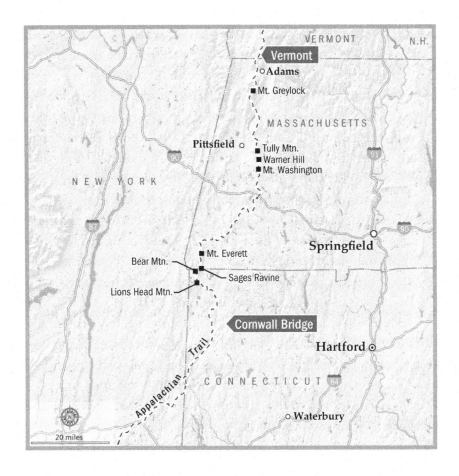

climbed the mountain to investigate the magical source of light he had seen from town below, and he finds an orphaned, isolated girl who had been wondering from afar about a similar curious light coming from his house down below. For Thoreau, the mountain woman had "lively sparkling eyes" and was "full of interest in the lower world from which I had come" and he thinks of "returning to this house, which was well kept and so nobly paced, the next day, and perhaps remaining a week there, if I could have entertainment." Scholars would wonder for decades to come about the opposing views of Greylock, of nature represented by a woman on a mountain. But rare would be the conversation about why both female characters were stagnant and isolated from the world below.

Here came another sojourner, more than a century later, this time a woman with the wind at her back, summiting Greylock at noon and finding a mountaintop restaurant where she sat to enjoy a hamburger, a glass of milk, and, for dessert, a bowl of ice cream, before making her descent toward North Adams and bedding down in the wild beside the trail, completely comfortable.

She continued through the Berkshires the next day, and randomly three high school boys and six girls joined her as she ventured through a valley and into the forest. They were talking and laughing as Emma told them about her trip.

I wish my grandmother was like you, said one of the girls.

Emma felt like the Pied Piper of Hamelin.

Around dusk, the girls headed back, but the boys continued walking with Emma. They led her to a freshwater spring and collected leaves to make her a bed nearby. Then they wished her well and headed back up the trail. She wrote about the boys and girls in her diary, and how much fun she'd had, and she relaxed on the leaves and finally found sleep.

— — — — —

That night as she dreamed, eight hundred miles to the south, monstrous waves began licking the coast between Myrtle Beach, South Carolina, and Wilmington, North Carolina. The tide surged five feet, six feet, seven feet—higher than normal—and the ravishing winds began flicking shingles off beach cottages and lifting boards from fishing piers and ripping tree limbs from branches. As the eye of the storm neared land it threw tornadoes across the low country, bouncing around South Carolina tobacco towns such as Conway, Latta, Dillon, and Bucksport, where one cut a swath two hundred yards wide and a quarter mile long, injuring a woman, her two daughters, and her son. Another twister dropped near Goldsboro, North Carolina, 150 miles north, damaging a tobacco barn and exploding the dwelling occupied by a man, his wife, and their three children, who were not injured.

Along the coast, evacuees by the thousands packed into churches and schools and other structures made of concrete farther inland. Farmers sealed up tobacco barns. Hospitals turned to auxiliary power. The navy secured its battleships. The National Guard evacuated two thousand coastal residents of New Bern, North Carolina, to higher ground. One hundred miles east of Boston, Massachusetts, construction workers were scurrying to sink and secure the massive legs of a radar island.

The storm slowed for a spell off the coast, sucking up moisture, cooling a little, and by the time the eye reached land near Morehead City, North Carolina, it was bursting with one-hundred-mile-per-hour winds and rainfall for the record books. It ripped off roofs and carried houses to sea. It chewed up fishing piers made of steel. And it slowly began to set a new course, turning toward the north, toward New England.

About twelve hundred miles behind the beast, closer to the equator, the winds of the second storm were quickly growing, and observers noticed a large cyclone circulating northeast of the Leeward Islands. They gave it a name: Tropical Storm Diane. A reconnaissance plane flying over the new storm measured steady gusts nearing fifty miles per hour and intensifying.

— — — — — —

Rain was falling when Emma woke, trailside, early on August 11. She hiked alone in the morning and was quickly soaked through, head to sneaker. She sloshed across the state line, leaving Massachusetts behind and entering Vermont on the Long Trail through the Green Mountains, toward the higher and more rugged section of the Appalachians, and the path was made horrible by the rain. Her shoes picked up mud and made walking hard and dangerous at times. In the afternoon she was joined by a pack of Boy Scouts; she didn't mind the company so she kept pace with the teens. She noticed one of their leaders occasionally watching her walk, as if he were studying the old woman's gait for lessons. After a while, he spoke up. He complimented Emma on her walking, and said her energy and determination to finish what she had started were admirable. She liked to hear that.

The Boy Scouts broke off and Emma hiked alone for a stretch, the clouds still soaking the earth, finally coming to a shelter near a mountain pond. Two young men, in their early twenties, had already claimed the little cabin for the night. They'd started a fire and were cooking dinner when she walked in, sopping wet. They didn't seem too happy to see her come along, but it was obvious there was no way she was leaving.

Harold Bell had just gotten out of the navy and Steve Sargent had left the US Naval Academy at Annapolis. They were hiking the Long Trail from Massachusetts to Killington, Vermont, doing some fishing and exploring along the way. They were surprised to see an elderly woman on this rugged, isolated section of trail, but they invited her in and made small talk. The young men were blown away that she had hiked all the way from Georgia, and even more surprised that she was carrying a shoulder sack that weighed less than twenty pounds. For ten days of hiking, the navy boys had each packed fifty-five-pound backpacks, and they felt a little foolish.

When it was time for bed, they hung blankets from the ceiling to divide the room. Like many of those Emma met along the trail, the young men would remember her for the rest of their lives, because of that chance meeting, and even more so because of what would happen a few days later, when they saw her again.

11

SHELTER

That Friday was the rainiest August day in the written history of New York City. And what was left of Hurricane Connie, which made landfall at Morehead, North Carolina, before scraping up the Atlantic Coast, had just begun its onslaught in the Northeast. Ten people in the metropolis already were dead from the floods, a number that would continue to climb. Between midnight Thursday and midnight Friday, Connie dumped nearly six inches of rain on New York. Faced with flooding in various parts of the city, sixty thousand volunteers in New York's civil defense program were on standby. The headline in the *New York Times* read, CONNIE BLOWS NORTH WITH FORCE EQUAL TO THOUSANDS OF H-BOMBS.

Behind the storm was a path of waterlogged destruction. In Wilmington, North Carolina, city hall was flooded by eighteen inches of water. Near Hampton Roads, Virginia, hurricane winds had slammed two freighters together. Seventy Red Cross shelters in the Carolinas held 14,756 refugees. Much of the tobacco and corn crop had been ruined.

At North Beach, Maryland, a young woman staggered out of the choppy Chesapeake Bay and collapsed on shore, and locals sounded an alarm. Wreckage from a sixty-four-year-old schooner called the *Levin J. Marvel*, which had been carrying tourists on a cruise, began to wash up. By the end of the day, a coroner had laid out ten bodies, still wearing life preservers, at the North Beach fire station.

Behind Connie, too, was another storm. In the darkness between August 11 and 12, the season's fourth hurricane curved abruptly to the northeast and picked up speed. The intensification was so rapid that overnight the winds increased from 50 miles per hour to 125 miles per hour.

The rain bands north of Connie covered virtually all of New England, dropping eight inches of rain on Connecticut in just two days. To the north, the rain running off the Green Mountains and White Mountains rapidly filled brooks and streams, which began to crest their banks and picked up velocity as they flowed downhill and fed into larger creeks and rivers.

Two hundred miles north of soaked New York City, Emma woke in a cabin in the woods, happy to have dry clothes thanks to the little fire. The navy boys were planning on sticking around the cabin to do some fishing, so she bade them good-bye and headed down the trail in a light rain. In the daybreak she could see that the nearby pond had swollen during the night and was pouring out over the trail. A wooden bridge across the stream was now a series of floating logs and she got her feet wet immediately while trying to get across. She wore a plastic cape around her shoulders but soon realized it was no use trying to stay dry. Minutes into her hike her clothes were soaked, and the wetter her sack got, the heavier her haul.

She had heard about a nice, well-kept shelter on Bromley Mountain, and for most of the hike she fantasized about getting out of the rain, drying her clothes, and having a hot bite to eat. In the late afternoon, when she came into a clearing and saw the shelter, Emma stopped in her tracks and gaped. Even from the outside, it appeared to be the most down-at-the-heels place she could imagine. To begin with, the lodge was abandoned. The doors were off their hinges and the windows had been broken out. When she stepped inside, rain was pouring through holes in the roof. Porcupines had eaten big chunks out of the wood floors. The stove was unusable.

She hung her wet clothes on an old ladder and stretched it over a fireplace. She got a fire going to dry out her things, but everything was so wet that she couldn't build enough heat. Disappointed though she was, she made the best of her surroundings. The water pouring in from a big hole in the roof made a decent stream in which she washed her clothes. Her sleep was intermittent. She couldn't keep dry in bed that night, due to the leaks.

— — — — — —

In July 1939, P. C. Gatewood sold his second farm and announced to his family that they were moving to Barkers Ridge, West Virginia, where he had bought an even smaller patch of land on which he hoped to grow tobacco. The farm was in disrepair and the fences needed work, but a log cabin sat on the property and there was room for a few sheep. Emma did not want to leave Ohio, but there was no use in fighting. So they packed their things into the truck and moved across the river, eighteen miles east of Huntington. She cried quietly the whole way.

The three children still living at home—Nelson, fifteen; Louise, thirteen; and Lucy, eleven—enrolled in school, and Emma got a job as a government monitor, her role to make certain no farmer planted more tobacco than he was allowed. She tried to make the best of her new life. She braided rugs and planted vegetables and found time to write poetry, rhymes that seemed to be longing for a better situation. She mailed back one untitled poem to her home newspaper in Gallipolis, which published it.

> A home is made of many things,
> Books and papers and little strings,
> A comb and brush to fix one's hair,
> A mending basket, and easy chair.
> A clock, some music, the Sacred Book,
> A kitchen stove and food to cook.
> The sound of little feet about
> Up the stairs, and in and out.
> Little trinkets on the floor,
> Trains and cars and dolls galore.
> Children's clothes and children's beds,
> A kitty cat that must be fed.
> A dog to warn us with his bark,
> When someone bothers when it's dark.
> A mother that is kind and good,
> And patient with her little brood.
> A great big place must Father fill,
> Besides the paying of the bills.
> A Spirit there that brings together,
> In every trial and kind of weather.
> There must be kindness every day,
> If it's a home with shining ray.

P.C. burned a mountain field and planted a small crop. Each Saturday morning, P.C. would leave with Armster Kingery and would not return until Sunday evening. His wife never asked him where he had been because she did not care.

It was on a Sunday in early September 1939 that Emma Gatewood received her last beating at the hands of her husband. It was then that her endurance of his cruelty ended.

The details can't be found in the various biographical sketches that accompanied the honors bestowed upon her in later years. They are not found in any newspaper article or magazine story about her either, and there are hundreds. In fact, the woman who did not smoke or drink or curse would tell newspaper reporters she was a widow for years to come, even if P. C. Gatewood was alive and well in Ohio. The details of this dark time were kept by her family, and they did not speak often of it for many years.

That September day, P.C. and Emma got into an argument that developed into their final fight. No one remembers what subject prompted the disagreement, and there is naturally some confusion about the order of events. What is known is that Nelson, fifteen, found his father assaulting his mother inside the home. He had beaten her in the face, which was swollen and bruised. Her upper and lower teeth were broken. Her left ear was black and a mole above her ear was ripped nearly off. One of her ribs was cracked.

Nelson, who had always been small for his age but was nearing 150 pounds of bone and muscle, grabbed his father, pinning P.C.'s arms to his sides, and lifted him off the floor. He told his mother to run and she did, out the front door and into the woods. Nelson held his father for a few more seconds, then released him, and P.C. ran in pursuit of his wife. When he couldn't find her, he returned and walked past Nelson to the stove, where he picked up an iron poker and raised it over his head.

Make your first swing a good one, Nelson told his father. *You're only going to get one.*

The old man didn't swing.

P.C. left that day, and Emma returned to the house in his absence. When he came back later, he was trailed by a deputy sheriff or justice of the peace. Some family members believe that P.C.'s friend, Armster Kingery, who held political clout in the region, pulled some strings to have Emma arrested. Whatever the case, P.C. parked his truck, climbed out, and walked purposefully toward the house, the lawman tagging behind. When he jerked open the front door, his wife was waiting with a five-pound sack of flour, which she heaved in his direction. The flour connected squarely with her husband's face and exploded into a cloud of white.

The four witnesses disagree about minor details, such as whether the flour incident occurred in the presence of the officer or preceded his arrival, but they collectively recall that Lucy and Louise were in a state of consternation. As the lawman walked their mother to his car, Louise ran inside to fetch her pocketbook. Lucy clung to her mother until the officer pulled her away.

The deputy placed Emma into his car and drove her to the neighboring town of Milton, West Virginia, where she was booked on unknown charges and locked inside a jail cell. She had held her own, come what may.

— — — — — —

Her shoes were wet. Her socks were wet. Her dungarees were wet. Her shirt was wet. Her sack was wet. When she left the Bromley shelter early the morning of August 13, rain was still falling.

Hurricane Connie had dumped record amounts of water on its course along the coast, the giant outer bands of its counterclockwise rotation dragging water from the Atlantic onto the land, and now it was moving toward the Great Lakes region. At 10:00 AM, the storm crossed the southeastern border of Pennsylvania, sideswiping New England and slashing a diagonal track across the Keystone State, the calm eye passing Harrisburg, over Pittsburgh and slightly northeast of Erie, before moving over Lake Erie and toward Ontario in Canada. The winds had slowed to fifty-five miles per hour, and weathermen had begun referring to Connie as a storm rather than a hurricane.

Still, the rain came.

In two days, the storm had dumped more than nine inches of rain on New York City, bringing train traffic at Grand Central Terminal to a halt for hours. Much of Connecticut got eight inches. Power and telephone service was out for many in the region. The northern Appalachian Mountains, the Whites, Greens, Taconics, and Alleghenies were all saturated, and their streams were running wild, sending incredible amounts of water rushing downhill into the Schuylkill and Delaware Rivers in Pennsylvania, the Delaware and Ramapo Rivers in New Jersey, the Delaware and Neversink Rivers in New York, the Potomac River in Virginia and Maryland, the Westfield River in Massachusetts, and the Naugatuck and Mad Rivers in Connecticut. Many of them were close to the flood stage, and there was another erratic storm a few days behind and headed north.

On the Appalachian Trail through Green Mountain National Forest, Emma was not walking so much as wading, and atop the ridges the wind—remnants of the hurricane—was blowing strong. She steeled herself against the elements and trudged onward. For nine miles she sloshed through water, strong winds, and driving rain. She ducked out of the deluge at a little shelter near Mad Tom Notch and had a soggy lunch from her sack. She hiked on through the afternoon at a much slower pace than she would have liked until she came to another shelter, at Griffith Lake, a small pond near Peru Peak. The shelter was occupied by a group of young black men and two slightly older white leaders from a Roman Catholic parish in Harlem. The men explained that they'd come up for a wilderness trip and had found themselves stuck inside because of the storm.

Emma enjoyed their company, though she was surprised to see them on the trail. She read the newspapers every day, so she was

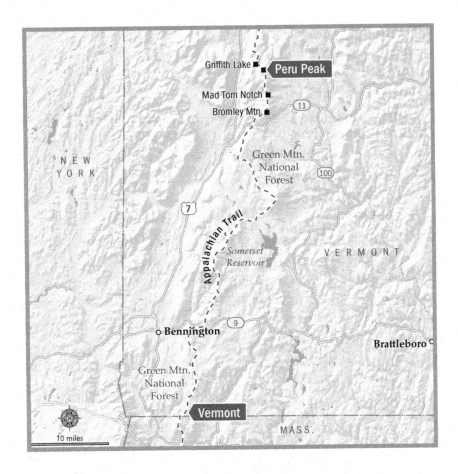

well aware of the tension between the races in 1955, when one in ten US citizens was black.

The previous May, the Supreme Court had outlawed separation of the races in public schools and launched a period of protest. It would be four months before the name Rosa Parks would enter the national conversation, but sparks of rebellion had begun to flare all over America as the federal government started to act in favor of equality. The Federal Trade Commission ruled that segregation in depot waiting rooms and on trains engaged in interstate transportation was illegal. A federal appeals court in Georgia, where the former governor wrote that "God advocates segregation," demanded Atlanta open its public golf courses to black golfers. A court in Richmond, Virginia, barred segregation on city buses.

In many places, the advancements implemented by the government strengthened the resolve of whites to maintain the upper hand. In South Carolina, a Negro Little League baseball team won its way to the state championship, then found that fifty-five competing white teams had withdrawn. In Arkansas, a Baptist congregation fired a pastor who preached against segregation. In Miami, a group of politically prominent African Americans was thrown out of a hotel after it had arrived, by invitation, to an Abraham Lincoln birthday dinner held by local Republicans. And White Citizens' Councils, a less secretive and less violent version of the Ku Klux Klan, sprouted across the South to put political and social pressure on blacks who tried to assert their new rights.

Emma talked to the young men a while, telling them of her trip, and decided to press on since staying the night would have made the eight-by-twenty-foot shelter a little too crowded. She walked down an embankment and came to a rushing creek near Little Mond Pond. She couldn't cross there, so she hiked up into the woods until she found a log stretched across the flowing water. She balanced carefully and made it across without falling. She walked down the trail a bit more and found that a flooded brook had joined the trail at a flat, narrow stretch. The water was running a mill race straight down the path. She stepped into the flow, but the water came all the way to her knee on the very first step, so she backed out. The shelter with the group from Harlem would have to do.

Emma came from a place that was nearly all white and completely segregated, but she did not discriminate. She taught her children to respect others, no matter their skin color or stage in life. She would not allow them to utter racial epithets and taught them to treat people as they wished to be treated themselves. One experience on the trail defined this attitude: An African American couple invited her to dinner, and when she was seated and served, they withdrew. She refused to eat unless they joined her, and she seemed embarrassed by their treatment.

— — — — — —

Emma found the boys baking two pones of cornbread. They had fashioned a little stove and were cooking over hot ashes from a fire. When they finished, they ate one cake and saved the other to eat on the trail the next day.

When it was time for bed, Emma squeezed herself into one corner and ducked under her blanket as the rain plinked off the roof. Before she dozed off, the young man next to her, apparently asleep, slung his arm across her body. She moved his limp appendage back. He did it again. She moved it back. He did it again.

Six days before, the Reverend G. W. Lee, a respected minister and local official of the National Association for the Advancement of Colored People, was killed by an unknown assailant in Belzoni, Mississippi. Seven days later, Emmett Till, a fourteen-year-old Chicago boy visiting family in Money, Mississippi, would be kidnapped and murdered and dumped in the Tallahatchie River after he allegedly whistled at a white woman. That very same day, August 13, a black man named Lamar Smith was shot to death in broad daylight within sight of the courthouse in Brookhaven, Mississippi, and police wouldn't be able to find a single witness to testify against the white men charged in his death.

And on the Appalachian Trail, inside a crowded little shelter in the Green Mountains of Vermont, an old white woman fell asleep under the arm of a young black man from Harlem.

12

I'LL GET THERE

AUGUST 14–15, 1955

Her sons were strong swimmers, and when they'd finished working in the tobacco fields, they'd race off toward the Ohio River and plunge into the cool water, washing away the day's dust and sweat. It was a good distance to the opposite bank, but when they were up to the challenge they could tear across the river and reach the other side, as if they were born with gills.

Their mother could not swim. She'd never learned how. If you dropped her into the Ohio, she could probably keep her head above water for a few moments out of sheer grit and determination, but she lacked the fundamentals of buoyancy.

She never spoke to her family of the months she spent preparing to hike the Appalachian Trail, but they'd later learn from friends and acquaintances in southern Ohio that Emma was often seen in the woods in advance of her journey. Her children would learn that she secretly made overnight expeditions to the wilderness to determine what equipment was completely necessary, what foods were lightweight and would help her maintain energy, and what first-aid supplies she might need in an emergency.

Despite those hours spent in forethought, she had never picked up the skill that would have proved mildly comforting at least on August 14, as the creeks and streams in the Green Mountains continued to rise.

Emma set out at about 8:00 AM with the young men from Harlem and their leaders, and they waded through water to their knees for much of the trail that morning, coming eventually to a fast-moving creek that was fifteen feet wide. They gradually stepped into the water, which came above Emma's knees. They slowly worked their way across, the leaders keeping a close eye on the young men. They used walking sticks to brace themselves against the swift current until they'd each made it to safety.

A short time later, they came to Ten Kilns Brook, which intersected the trail, and this stream was swollen as well, twenty feet from bank to bank. In the middle was a large rock, and the water between them and the rock wasn't flowing as rapidly as it was beyond the rock. The leaders went first, carefully maneuvering to the other side. Then the boys started, walking first to the rock then grabbing hold of a pole held by one of the leaders and inching the rest of the way across against the heavy flow.

Emma was last. She baby-stepped through the calmer water to the rock, then heaved her pack across to one leader and gripped the pole for the rough stretch. When she stepped into the swift water, it nearly took her feet from under her. She held tight to the pole and kept moving, feeling the creek bottom with her feet, trying to keep her balance, until she reached the other side.

The rain stopped that morning. The sun burned down. Emma's soaked clothes began to dry, and gradually things seemed a little better. The group stopped at Old Job Shelter for lunch, and the boys laughed as they pelted green apples off a nearby tree. A few hours of hiking later, their clothes had dried completely, and they walked across a rustic wooden bridge to a shelter on a little island. It was a beautiful spot where the mirrored waters of Little Rocky Pond, stocked full with rainbow trout, reflected mountains covered by evergreens.

Emma thought about staying. She would have liked to, but she needed to make progress after a slow and miserable last couple of days. She said good-bye to the group from Harlem, picked up her pace, and put in seven more miles through farmland and a long patch of lowlands before bedding down for the night at Buffum Shelter. She logged the experience in her diary, adding: "The boys, all but one colored, were very nice."

There is no other mention of them in her journals, and one might easily assume from the paragraphs dedicated to the chance encounter that the boys were simply Roman Catholic youths on a wilderness journey. Their story was lost for decades. But before his death in 2010, one of the white leaders would recount meeting Emma Gatewood on the trail. Rev. Dr. David Loomis wrote this version of those few wet days:

> The summer I turned 21, I worked for a church in East Harlem, New York, which had the highest density of population on earth at that time and a murder rate to prove it. Each square inch of concrete was fought over by gangs, with summer's heat adding fuel to that fire.
>
> In hopes of brokering peace between the two largest rival gangs, the church I worked for had me take the four top

honchos of each gang for a week-long hike along the Appalachian Trail in Vermont. None of the eight could resist the church's invitation to take an all-expenses-paid vacation far from the heat of the city.

Our first day out, we hiked 15 miles out before a hurricane unexpectedly blew inland and trapped us inside an 8 x 20 foot trailside lean-to. As night fell, Emma Gatewood, a 5'2" grandma who was living her dream of hiking the entire trail from Georgia to Maine staggered into camp. Bruised, exhausted, her gear and provisions washed away by swollen streams, she was in dire need. What made things tricky was that Emma was a genteel white Southern lady. She could hide neither her drawl nor her unease at living in close proximity to eight young black males, her distress leading all eight to bestow on her their stoniest stares.

It rained and blew hard. . . . The brute force of nature so overwhelmed us it literally dissolved the tension in our lean-to. That hurricane, by facing us with a severe, totally mutual challenge, forced us all back to what we had in common, our humanity. Like people trapped in a lifeboat, we came together to try to stay afloat. We took turns standing by a fire we had built by breaking off dead branches, thereby freeing up enough floor space for five of us to stretch out and sleep. We also took turns getting drenched collecting more deadwood.

Hiking out once the rains let up, Emma piggybacked on a variety of youthful backs as we forded swollen torrents that would have swept her downstream had she attempted them on her own. Whoever she was piggybacking on had somehow to stay balanced mid-stream while enduring a tight, often suffocating neck squeeze from her two thin, bony arms.

— — — — — —

Mary Snow's story about Emma ran in *Sports Illustrated* on August 15—the day Emma would face death—under a black-and-white photograph of her on the trail. The headline was: PAT ON THE BACK.

> A 67-year-old great-grandmother, Mrs. Emma Gatewood of Gallipolis, Ohio, is determined to be the first woman to hike the entire length of the Appalachian Trail, 2,050 miles of mountain footpath from Mt. Oglethorpe, Georgia, to Mt. Katahdin, Maine. Mrs. Gatewood, alone and without a map, began following the white blaze marks of the trail early in May, and this week from Connecticut's Cathedral Pines, Grandmother Gatewood could look back on 1,500 miles of the best and worst of nature. She had carefully avoided disturbing three copperheads and two rattlesnakes on the trail, flipped aside one attacking rattler with a walking stick. When caught without nearby shelter she had heated some stones and slept on them to keep from freezing. For snacks Grandma nibbled wild huckleberries, young sorrel for salad and sucked bouillon cubes to combat loss of body salt.
>
> Her contacts with other humans ranged from a miserly individual who refused her even a drink, to a generous housewife who supplied fried chicken to carry on the trail.
>
> Mrs. Gatewood is serenely confident that she can finish her trek. "I'll get there except if I break something loose. And when I get atop Mt. Katahdin, I'll sing *America, The Beautiful*, 'From sea to shining sea.'"

— — — — — —

She could go no farther.

She had started at 6:00 AM and faced a wicked, weedy trail all morning before coming to Clarendon Gorge. This one was wider than the others, forty feet from bank to bank, wide enough to necessitate a bridge even when the creek wasn't flooded. The old bridge had burned some time ago and a temporary bridge had been fashioned, but rains from the storm had washed the new bridge out. There was no way she could cross.

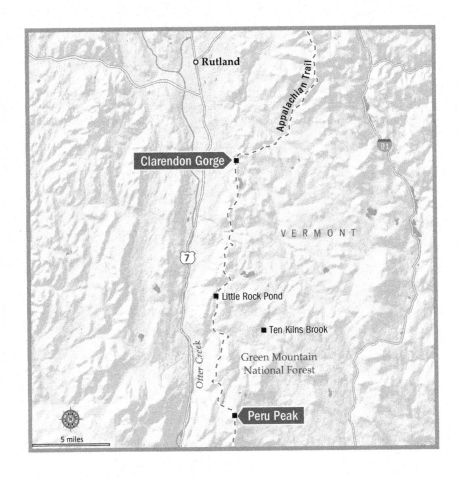

She walked up the gorge a ways and found a spot that she estimated was only about three feet deep, but the water was moving
so swiftly that she wasn't about to try it alone. She hollered into
the woods to see if anybody was within earshot. Maybe there was
a chance someone nearby knew where she could get across. She got
no response. She was all alone, and she was stuck.

She removed the damp clothes from her sack and laid them out
in the sun to dry. If she was going to be forced to wait, at least she
could be productive and lighten her load a bit. She spread out her
blanket, too, and decided to catch a little sun. After days of gray,
cloud-covered skies, the warm light was welcome.

And she waited. Nobody came by noon, or by one o'clock, or
by two, or by three. Long hours she spent idle. Then, around four
o'clock, she heard someone coming. She stood and peered down the
trail and saw who it was: Howard Bell and Steve Sargent, the two
boys she had met several days before. The navy boys. She couldn't
have planned it better. She was surprised, and very happy to see
those two.

They'd had a rough go. What started as a nice little outdoor
break from the navy had turned into a wet and soppy journey. It had
rained eight out of the nine days they'd been on the trail, so much
that their feet were blistered and they were miserable.

Emma told them about her predicament and walked them
down to the gorge that was now so wide and flowing so fast. The
young men inspected the water and decided they could wade across
if they took some precautions. They walked back to where they
had dropped their backpacks. One of the boys fished a big bunch of
parachute cord from his. He tied Emma's sack securely to the top of
his big, heavy backpack, then tied a length of cord around his waist.
The other young man tied a cord around his own waist and they
walked down to the water's edge.

Emma stood between them and they looped the cord around her waist, tying her firmly in the middle, a human sandwich. When the knots were tight, the boys each took one of her hands and they began to slowly wade against the roaring current. The water inched past their knees, then their waists, then up to their chests, beating hard against their bodies. They strained against the current. Emma closed her eyes, feeling the stone riverbed with her feet, trying for all she was worth to hold on. Step by slippery, precarious step.

Her head was swimming. She opened her eyes, but couldn't look at the current that was trying to suck her downstream. She tilted her chin back and stared up at the sky instead, and squeezed the boys' hands.

One of the young men, Sargent, would say fifty-seven years later that he was so scared crossing that river that he still visited it in his dreams at the age of seventy-nine. "We were touch and go getting across," he would say. The other, Bell, would recall how fast the water was flowing, and how he felt that one misstep would send them all rushing downstream, tangled in rope. They'd both come back decades later to hike the same ground, and they'd fondly remember Emma's friendly, determined nature. "She was one tough old bird," Bell would say.

That day, though, there in the middle of the rushing water, so close to catastrophe, Emma Gatewood laughed out loud at how ridiculous it was that a sixty-seven-year-old woman had gotten herself into such a predicament.

They finally reached dry ground and scrambled up the bank. She ducked into woods to change from her wet Bermuda shorts and back into her dungarees.

"Well," she said, reappearing, "you got grandma across."

13

DESTRUCTION

The folks at the Long Trail Lodge were expecting her, and when Emma arrived at the hotel near Killington, Vermont, that afternoon, they fixed her a sandwich in the kitchen then put her on the phone with a reporter from the *Rutland Herald*. Rutland was about nine miles west.

It seemed like the whole country wanted to know what she was up to now, and reporters were following her every move. If the first three-quarters of the journey had been considered a novel attempt at greatness by an eccentric old lady, now that she was on the home stretch, she had captured the attention of the country. An Associated Press dispatch went out the next day, reporting that Emma had lost twenty-four pounds and worn out five pairs of shoes. "So far she has walked 1700 miles," the article read, "with about 350 miles more to go to Mt. Katahdin."

Three hundred fifty miles left. What the article didn't mention was that the miles before her were some of the most difficult, perilous miles on the trail. She had faced cold nights in the South in the spring, but there were nights ahead when the temperature would drop below freezing and the skies would spit stinging sleet. She'd averaged roughly fifteen miles a day so far, but her daily mileage would be cut to a third of that once she reached the White Mountains of New Hampshire, just ahead. And as northbound

hikers before her had learned, there were long stretches, including the daunting 100 Mile Wilderness, which were so isolated and inaccessible that carrying enough food to survive for a week or more was a necessity.

Emma figured she might as well get started.

She followed the narrowest path she'd encountered so far—"About like a squirrel would use," she thought—up and over and around some boulders and into Gifford Woods State Park. Earl V. Shaffer stayed at the same park seven years before, on his inaugural thru-hike in 1948. "There I signed the register, then talked to Grace Barrows, the first and only lady Ranger met on the Long Cruise," Shaffer wrote later. "She told me that the lean-tos in the Park were available at a nominal fee. But several hours of daylight remained and I decided to keep going. Mrs. Barrows misunderstood and always blamed herself for my going. She told me years later that she never charged a through-hiker after that, regardless of regulations."

Alas, when Emma arrived, Mrs. Barrows, conflicted, said she did not like to charge, but as it was a state park she was required to charge a dollar. Emma didn't mind and fetched a dollar from her pocket, even if she planned to sleep in the grass.

"To ease her conscience," Emma wrote in her journal, "she brought me a tray of hot baked potatoes, slices of ham, beets, bread, two slices of jelly roll, glass of milk, and hot coffee."

Mrs. Barrows mentioned that two young men had come off the trail and reserved the adjacent table on which to sleep. Emma was delighted to find it was the navy boys who helped her across the creek. She gave them her drip coffee, some crackers, a piece of jelly roll and some cookies to supplement their dinner. They all stayed awake a while talking and then Emma went to sleep on a big pile of leaves. In the night, she felt a couple of cold sprinkles on her face and she quickly grabbed her sack and headed to the porch of the caretaker's home. The boys trudged up onto the porch a few minutes later, good and wet. A few other men who had been working on the trail had made their beds on the tables, so Emma lay on the floor. Soon enough, the rain started falling harder and blowing under the overhang and the porch floor grew wetter by the minute. Emma climbed upon a table and the navy boys doubled up on another. None of them got much sleep.

As they dried their clothes over a fire early the next morning, Hurricane Diane was plunging into the East Coast eight hundred miles south, not far from where Hurricane Connie had made landfall five days before. The storm was packing winds of one hundred miles per hour near the eye and moving west at fourteen miles per hour, but observers were already saying that Diane wasn't going to cause nearly as much damage as Connie. Houses had been damaged by waves and streets were flooded in coastal towns, but the storm didn't pack the punch of its predecessor. It quickly began losing steam, so much so that hurricane warnings were expected to be called off that afternoon. What the forecasters weren't taking into account, however, was that the storm's path would keep it centered over the coast, so it continued to suck up moisture from the Atlantic and sling it inland, onto ground still saturated by Connie.

On the trail, the hikers were oblivious. News came by word of mouth, and with the Washington Weather Bureau downplaying the storm already, there wasn't any alarm, even when the storm started tracking north.

A volunteer who had been clearing the trail came with bad news: a beaver dam had caused flooding and the valley below was impassable. He knew Emma was hiking the trail, and he told her there was no way she could cross the flooded stretch. He offered to drive her around it and she accepted. Faced with an impassable obstacle, these two miles were the only on the A.T. she'd miss.

On August 18, Emma headed east toward the Connecticut River, the dividing feature between Vermont and New Hampshire, and in the evening she walked into a town called Hartland and looked for a store to stock up. She talked to the proprietor for a few minutes and he told her she could probably find her a place to stay about half a mile or so off the trail.

She followed his directions and was headed down the road when a car pulled up beside her. A woman asked Emma her name, then said they had been searching for her. The woman was Mrs. Ruetenik, and they were from Ohio. When they saw the newspaper story and realized Emma was so close and would be coming down the trail soon, they set out to find her. Mrs. Ruetenik asked if Emma needed a place to stay the night and offered her a bed in a cabin they were house-sitting for some friends. Emma accepted the invitation and piled in the car and rode with them a few miles to the mountainside home, which had a lovely view of the countryside. Mrs. Ruetenik had a baby and a few small children, but she didn't seem worried at all about her ragged company. She served Emma hot dogs and tomatoes as they sat outside and enjoyed the view.

Meanwhile, to the south, the outer bands of Hurricane Diane, which had been downgraded to a tropical storm, were dumping water on New England as they moved north. Nobody seemed too concerned about the menacing clouds, but they soon began to understand that the new rainfall was rapidly filling smaller rivers and streams. It wasn't until late in the afternoon that the first flash-flood warning was issued. As people across the region went to sleep to the sound of rain pattering their roofs, the water began to rise.

— — — — — —

The mayor of Milton, West Virgina, didn't know Emma's history, didn't know about P.C. or the decades of abuse or the details of their final fight, but he knew a battered spouse when he saw one. And he knew that a fifty-three-year-old woman with broken teeth and a cracked rib did not belong in jail.

He talked to her for a while and felt sorry for her. The miscarriage of justice had to be corrected. He invited Emma to stay in his home, safe and protected, until she got back on her feet. He got her a job working in a restaurant for some spending money.

Back home, the children were in a state of confusion. Their mother had sent word that she was OK, and that they'd be together soon, but the three still at home—Nelson, Louise, and Lucy—didn't know what to expect next.

They got up early one morning and, with the help of a few neighbors, killed and cleaned a hog. They built a fire under a barrel of water and strung the hog up before it was time for the kids to go to school. When they arrived home from school that afternoon, their father was gone. P.C. had taken the bedroom sets and furniture and nearly everything they owned out of the house. There on the table was half of the hog carcass, a parting gift.

Nelson, the oldest still at home at fifteen, had been working as an assistant to the janitor at school and he had always been tight with his money. His older sister Esther once asked him if he'd like a little spending money, and when he said he would, she gave him a dime. A few weeks later, she asked him if he needed a little more and he replied, "No, I still got that dime." He had eventually saved up enough money to buy a Remington single-shot, bolt-action rifle and a bicycle with a headlight and fenders for twenty-six dollars from Montgomery Ward in Huntington. Now he found some pocket change and rode that new bicycle three miles to the general store, where he phoned his mother and told her that their father was gone.

You want me to stay and help get things straightened up tomorrow? he asked her.

No, go on to school, she said. *I'll be on the first bus.*

When the children stepped off the bus the next day, Emma greeted them. She had put the meat away and organized the house. She had taken care of everything and carried on without mentioning the recent chaos, as though she'd never left.

She was planning to ask a judge for a peace bond, which would require P.C. to keep his hands off her, but she learned that he had hired a lawyer to dispute her claims. So she hired a lawyer, too, and on September 6, 1940, at the big stone courthouse in Huntington, West Virginia, Emma Gatewood, after thirty-five years of matrimony, filed for divorce.

Five months later, on February 6, 1941, Emma and her lawyer appeared before a judge and divorce commissioner. Emma testified to the discord in her marriage, to the abuse she had suffered and the ways in which she had been mistreated. After consideration, the judge issued his decree: "That the bond of matrimony heretofore existing between the plaintiff, Emma R. Gatewood, and the defendant, P.C. Gatewood, is hereby dissolved and the said plaintiff is hereby granted an absolute divorce from the defendant from the bond of matrimony."

He awarded Emma custody of Louise, fourteen; Lucy, twelve; and Nelson, sixteen; and demanded that P.C. pay Emma fifteen dollars a month in alimony. He also awarded Emma the farm on Barkers Ridge and demanded that P.C. continue to make payments on it. If he failed to do that, he'd be called back to court.

Emma wrote later that she had been "happy ever since."

"I know when I go to bed that no brute of a man is going to kick me out into the floor and then lie out of it," she wrote.

But he wasn't done causing her grief. He would fail to pay monthly alimony and run up a debt of two hundred dollars. Then, when she threatened to sue, he'd promise to deed her the farm and give her half of what he owed.

But she could deal with that. Their relationship was finally over. He would never again lay a hand on her.

Portrait, age fifty-four, 1942.
Courtesy Lucy Gatewood Seeds

— — — — —

She crossed the Connecticut River into New Hampshire at Hanover and walked quickly through town, hoping that no one had alerted another newspaper reporter to her presence. She was beginning to tire of the consistent delays. To make matters worse, the reporter in Rutland a few days before had somehow gotten the idea that she intended to square-dance in front of the television cameras when she finished the trail. And CBS News had broadcast the error on television. She had no intention of square-dancing in private, much less in front of the American television-viewing public.

At least it wasn't raining in Hanover.

She didn't know it then, but the storm chasing Emma up the coast was causing massive devastation to the south as it slung a final black band of rain on New Jersey, New York, Pennsylvania, Connecticut, and Massachusetts. The storm had been nearly counted out by weathermen on Thursday; it looked like nothing more than a low-pressure system moving over New England. But it was still moving, rotating in a vast counterclockwise direction, sucking up warm and moisture-laden air from the Atlantic and pushing humidity in the Northeast to sultry, almost tropical levels. Then came a low-pressure trough. Wet air rose, cooled, expanded, and began falling across the region. Diane was not dead. Not yet.

In the early morning hours in Waterbury, Connecticut, where Emma had stopped to visit with Mrs. Clarence Blake two weeks before, floodwaters from the Naugatuck River had surged thirty-five feet in places, topping riverbanks and washing away bridges and homes, destroying businesses and sucking families into the raging water. Parents tied their children to treetops as they prayed for rescue. In Winsted, the serene Mad River smashed through town and isolated residents from rescuers. In Farmington, a rescue boat capsized, sending little Patricia Ann Bechard to her death, and a fireman lashed little Linda Barolomeo to a tree before he was washed into floodwaters himself. In Seymour, the water unearthed caskets from a graveyard and sent them bobbing downstream. In Putnam, a magnesium plant caught fire and shot flames 250 feet in the air. Everywhere, police and firefighters were rushing from house to house, ordering residents to get out. The entire town of Ellenville, New York, population four thousand, was evacuated. But for many, the warnings came too late.

The rainfall totals in Connecticut were unbelievable. Fourteen inches in Torrington. Thirteen in Winsted. Twelve in Hartford. Nearly twenty inches fell in Westfield, Massachusetts.

The worst episode was playing out in Stroudsburg, Pennsylvania, near the Delaware Water Gap. The usually gentle Brodhead Creek rose thirty feet in fifteen minutes, plunging into a religious retreat called Camp Davis, where the campers fled to a house on higher ground. As water rose, they climbed into the second story, then the attic, until the house gave a shudder and collapsed. One woman would recall hearing children screaming hysterically as she clung to debris. She would later learn that thirty-one campers were dead.

Stroudsburg was isolated for ten hours. Across the region, flooding rivers washed away seven bridges. A fleet of helicopters rescued 235 passengers from a stranded Lackawanna Railroad train in the Pocono Mountains. In nearby Milford, two men, tied together by ropes, found an elderly woman stranded in her apartment and carried her to safety.

President Eisenhower would declare six eastern states disaster areas in need of federal relief. The combined death toll for both storms would climb above two hundred and the damage would be estimated at well over $1.5 billion, the highest on record. But around noon on August 20, the rain began to subside and the rivers grudgingly receded toward normal channels. The flooding failed to spread much father north than Northampton, Massachusetts.

In Hanover, New Hampshire, where tourists had holed up in motels because routes to the south were flooded or impassable, Emma walked on through town, unaware of the death and chaos spread out behind her.

She saw a couple of girls playing tennis in a park in town and she asked them if they wanted to go on a hike. The girls didn't answer and Emma continued down the road. Two blocks later, she heard someone running up behind her. The girls had followed her. They wanted to know if she was the woman hiking from Georgia to Maine who they had heard about.

Emma told them who she was. She asked if they knew of a place to eat outside town, but they didn't. One of the girls insisted Emma come home with her to have lunch. Emma thought the girl's mother might be upset by a surprise guest, but she followed them back to the courts anyway. The mother was somewhat taken aback, but she made the best of it and drove them all home for sandwiches.

When her husband walked in the front door, he shook Emma's hand like he knew her. She didn't know why until he fetched his copy of *Sports Illustrated*. She had not yet seen the story, so she read it there. The man, Dr. Lord, phoned a friend who belonged to the Dartmouth Outing Club and asked if Emma could stay in one of their cabins along the trail. His friend was receptive. He said the trail was clean most of the way to the cabins and that she'd find them easily.

After lunch, Dr. Lord drove Emma back to where she had left the trail. When she got to the outskirts of town, a woman and some teenagers were there, waiting to meet her. They visited for a while and when Emma decided it was time to press on, the teenagers, two girls and three boys, rode their bikes beside her down the road for two miles. One of the girls insisted on carrying Emma's sack in her bike basket.

Emma never found the "clean" trail that Dr. Lord's friend had mentioned. Instead, she hiked through weeds that stretched well above her head. When she came to a clearing, she noticed that an envelope had been pinned to a post beside the trail. Upon closer inspection, her name was written on the envelope. Inside was a note from a woman who lived in a red house just off the trail. The woman wanted to invite Emma in for tea.

The invitation made her happy. She felt like a dignitary. She joined the woman for dinner, then the woman's husband, George Bock, told Emma how to get inside the Dartmouth Outing Club cabins. She arrived before dark and got a good night's rest on a real mattress.

At noon the next day, as she came to a highway, she spotted a man waiting with camera gear.

You boys always seem to find me, she said.

He introduced himself as a photographer, Hanson Carroll, from the nearby *Valley News*. He had been trying to track her down for a few hours. He first heard she had come through Hanover that morning, so he talked to Burdette Weymouth at the Hanover Information Booth, who showed him where the trail went up and over Moose Mountain. Not being endowed with the same energies as Emma, Carroll drove around Moose Mountain and waited along Lyme-Dorchester Road for her to come out of the woods. Within an hour, she came down the hill and into the road, tan and smiling.

He asked Emma whether she would mind if he took a few photographs and filmed her hiking. She said she didn't. He took what must've been a hundred feet of film, shots of Emma eating lunch by the trail sign, walking along the road with two little girls and a boy, walking alone. She told him she had already worn out five pairs of sneakers. She was wearing her sixth. They talked about all the attention she was receiving and he asked her if it bothered her. She explained that she was not adverse to publicity, so long as the reporters didn't take up too much of her time.

He got the hint, but he asked her one more question.

Why are you doing this?

Just for the heck of it, she said.

— — — — — —

Hanson Carroll's story ran in the *Valley News* on Monday, August 22, 1955. Its place on the front page was a curious, haunting reminder of how close Emma Gatewood had been to danger.

The bold headline at the top of the front page read: PESTILENCE THREATENED AS FLOOD'S TOLL IS COUNTED. The smaller headline read: DAMAGE THOUGHT TO BE MORE THAN $1 BILLION; EIGHTY-SIX KNOWN DEAD.

Below the headline was a photograph of Emma, smiling, sitting in the grass and touching a sign that said APPALACHIAN TRAIL. Below the photograph was another headline: GRANDMA WALKS APPALACHIAN TRAIL FOR "THE HECK OF IT"

14

SO MUCH BEHIND

Emma woke in the dark atop Mount Cube, its open ledges offering spectacular views both back down over the valley toward Hanover and to the north toward Mount Moosilauke and the White Mountains. She stood atop the pinkish-gray quartzite, which reminded her of granite or marble, and looked out upon what many hikers considered the most rugged part of the trail.

Besides the dangerous terrain, the White Mountains—and the Presidential Range in particular—were famous for unpredictable, erratic, wicked weather. The range was the collision point for several valleys that funneled winds from the west, southwest, and south. It was also at the center of multiple storm tracks that brought weather from the Great Lakes, the Appalachian Valley, and the Atlantic.

"The Highlands of New Hampshire have a bleak ruggedness that commands the respect of the hardiest mountaineer," wrote Earl V. Shaffer, in *Walking with Spring*, his book about his inaugural thru-hike in 1948. "Some of the worst weather on earth occurs here, with winds of more than gale velocity and temperatures of polar intensity. Freezing weather is possible in midsummer and a snowstorm can follow hot weather within an hour. . . . The results can be overwhelming. Many people have died because they didn't know or ignored these facts. Precautions should be taken. Scanty clothing should never be worn above timberline and emergency rations and gear should be carried."

Emma looked out on the horizon, toward Mount Washington, the highest peak in the northeast at 6,288 feet. Though not impressive compared to the world's tallest peaks, the mountain's blustery weather—with year-round temperatures averaging below freezing and average winds blowing at thirty-five miles per hour—had caught many hikers off-guard. The highest wind speed ever recorded—231 miles per hour—was atop Mount Washington, twenty years before. Winds blew so steadily stiff that shelters had to be chained and anchored to the earth.

Hikers there had died from hypothermia, drowning, falling ice, avalanches, and falls. Two men, one in 1890 and the other in 1912, left the mountaintop on hikes and were never seen again. The year before her hike, two men died of hypothermia. The year after, two men would fall to their deaths, and one would be killed by an avalanche. By the time she arrived, some twenty-five people had perished on the mountain and scores of others had to be rescued.

Emma didn't have any of the proper gear that Shaffer referred to, but what she brought in her sack had served her fine so far. She had been able to wash out some things the night before. She had also been greeted that night by a porcupine, a big thing, which came sniffing around her feet. She gave it a kick and thought it was gone, but a little later the porcupine climbed up and got right in her face. She switched on her flashlight and he scooted away, never to return.

She set out that morning, coming down off Mount Cube on a series of shaky ladders, a new experience for her, but she managed just fine. She walked to a farmhouse near the base of the mountain and knocked on the door. Peter Thomson was eleven at the time, but he'd never forget the experience.

"My mother came and opened the door," he'd recall fifty-seven years later. "She said, 'Hi, my name is Emma Gatewood and I'm the first woman to walk the entire Appalachian Trail by herself.'" His mother invited the old woman in. Emma washed her hands and face and sat down to a home-cooked meal with the family. The two women would become good friends and pen pals, and Emma would visit several times in later years. She would inspire the elder Thomsons to take up hiking, and the couple would eventually summit all forty-six of the major Adirondack peaks, often accompanied by state troopers, for Meldrim Thomson Jr. would serve three terms as the mountain-loving governor of New Hampshire. His political success aside, for years to come he would open his home to Appalachian Trail thru-hikers, and his children would do the same, sending hikers on their way with maple syrup and a box of their mother's famous pancake mix.

In 1955, the man who would become governor took some pictures of his sons with Emma, and the boys followed her for quite a way down the trail to pick blackberries. She spent the night at Eliza Brook Shelter and hiked along a difficult, challenging stretch of trail the next day, climbing Mount Kinsman, then Mount Moosilauke, the most southern of the four-thousand-foot peaks in the White Mountains, where she came out above the timberline. The trail was marked by cairns, and the view across the bald boulder field was incredible. She didn't see a place to stay, so she followed a steep

Emma with Thomson brothers (from left) Tom, seven; David, nine; and Peter, eleven; near the Thomson home in Orford, New Hampshire, on her first thru-hike in 1955. Courtesy Peter Thomson

side trail that ran off the ridge, alongside Beaver Brook, and took her down seven treacherous ladders. She spent the night at a motel.

She climbed back to the trail the next morning and walked over Cannon Mountain, where she saw the Aerial Tramway gracefully whisking loads of people from bottom to top of the magnificent peak. A few of the tourists waiting in a small park at the summit gaped and snapped Emma's photograph, as if she were an animal from the wilderness, as she walked through. She climbed down to Franconia Notch in the evening, dropped her sack on the porch of the only house she could see, and walked to a nearby restaurant for dinner. When she returned to the house for her sack, the folks there had gone for the evening, before she could ask permission to stay. A boy had mowed the lawn earlier and had raked the grass into a big pile by the road. Emma waited until dark before she hustled over and carried three big loads of grass to a secluded spot by some bushes, where she fluffed it into a bed. She was one hundred feet from the road, at least, but she didn't want anyone to see her sleeping outside like a vagrant, so she pulled her blanket up over her body and covered it with grass for camouflage. She was warm on a cold night and slept well.

On August 25, she hiked to Lafayette Campground, then walked back a little ways on the highway for a good view of the Old Man of the Mountain, a set of granite outcroppings on a mountainside in the shape of a man's face. The great orator and statesman Daniel Webster once said about the outcropping, "Men hang out their signs indicative of their respective trades; shoe makers hang out a gigantic shoe; jewelers a monster watch, and the dentist hangs out a gold tooth; but up in the Mountains of New Hampshire, God Almighty has hung out a sign to show that there He makes men."

The old woman of the mountains kept climbing, up and up the steep ascent of bald rocks, and finally came to the Greenleaf Hut on Mount Lafayette, where she got a bite to eat before continuing on to Galehead Hut, kept tidy by two college students, caretakers there, who kindly prepared her dinner.

She walked to Zealand Falls Hut the next afternoon and got some food and raisins for the trail. She started again down the slope and walked a while before she realized she was lost. The trail was unmarked but clearly a trail, and so she kept going for several hours until she came to a little campground just as the sun was sliding behind the mountains. A man had set up camp there. When she explained her predicament, he offered to drive her back as far as he could, and she accepted. She walked a little farther in the night and slept beside the trail.

She made it the rest of the way back to the path the next morning and walked through a boggy plateau to Wiley House Station, then toward Mount Webster. The climb, from the beginning, was steep and rough. She came to a ladder where the rungs were so far apart that she had to plant one foot on the cliff face and pull herself up until she could get her knee over the next rung, then get her foot on it. It was difficult climbing.

A few miles later she came to a spot where the trail stretched alongside a bluff, so close to the edge of a cliff that she was afraid she'd fall off. Falling happened to be the number one cause of death in these parts. The wind was strong, too—giant gusts of cold air coming up the face of the cliff. She tried to time the gales, waiting for a break so she could shimmy across. She worked up her confidence and then went for it, between gusts, and she made it behind a clump of pine trees to safety.

She climbed Mount Jackson that afternoon, where she misread a trail sign and again took the wrong path. A woman she met on the trail put in a good word with the forest warden at Crawford Notch, and he let Emma stay the night with him.

The next morning, her knee was causing her pain, and though the days were bearably mild, the cold was slicing through the mountains at night. Emma knew she'd need extra provisions as August faded toward September. She made it to the scenic Lakes of the Clouds Hut, on the southern shoulder of Mount Washington, where she had lunch before summiting. The sky was bright and clear at the top and a large number of tourists had gathered to take in the sights. They gaped at the wrinkled, trail-stained woman suddenly in their presence. She wouldn't return the favor. Two boys walked up and sheepishly introduced themselves, then asked her questions about the trail.

She set off again for Mount Adams, following the trail as it bent along the crest of the Presidential Range, above the trees. Her knee was still bothering her and the trail was rugged. In the evening, as she approached Madison Spring Hut, she heard a group of men, women, and children talking and laughing. When she got close enough she could make out about fifteen people in the group. She knew they saw her, and suspected they had been waiting for her, but she sat down on a rock behind some evergreens, being coy. She decided she'd make them come to her, and before long, they did. They had been expecting her, and they brought out their cameras to take her picture.

One of the women, Ruth Pope, gave Emma a bandage for her knee. Another, Jean Lees, gave her some wool gloves and a ski hat, which Emma stowed in her sack. They made her feel welcome and treated her with respect and kindness. The hut master didn't even charge her the six dollars for a bunk, and she thanked him by giving him her green eyeshade, autographed.

She wrapped her knee in the morning, and the two women she met the night before volunteered to carry her sack. They broke off at Pinkham Notch and took a trail through Wildcat Mountains. When they found Emma again they were arguing about which one of them had carried the pack the longest. Emma reached Carter Notch after dark and accidentally stepped on her glasses. The frames were broken but she had brought along another pair, a lesson learned from her experience in Maine the year before.

She tackled another mountain the next day, twice, because she misread signs; she blamed her own ignorance and a poorly marked trail. Her mileage had slowed considerably as she neared the Maine state line on account of her injury, the brutal climbs, and the occasional misdirection. A boy in the woods set her on the right path that day, and by then it was raining again.

When she reached the hut in the evening, she couldn't believe her eyes. The hut master had made a huge meal, and she was hungry. On top of that, they didn't charge her anything for the meal or the bunk. All her clothes were wet, so she made a dress from a blanket by forming pleats with safety pins. She made it work and dried her clothes by the fire. She topped Carter Dome the following day, August 31, and found Imp Shelter, which had a stove and made for a nice place to spend the last night of August.

The next day she walked over Mount Moriah, onto the highway, and followed it into Gorham, New Hampshire, for supplies. She found supper and a nice bed at Androscoggin Inn, where Mrs. Tanner kept the big and beautiful white house.

She left Gorham early and walked over jagged and rocky trail the next day, over Mount Hayes and Cascade Mountain, by Passage Pond and Moss Pond, up over Mount Success, and then, without any fanfare, she crossed the state line into Maine, climbing Mount Carlo. As the sun faded, she realized she had missed the shelter down below. She found two boys on the top of the 3,565-foot peak, sitting on rocks, but as darkness fell they descended toward the shelter she must have missed. The night was pleasant, so she scouted out a place to sleep outdoors and found a thick bed of moss that was perfect, the kind of soft a rich man with a trick back would pay to have made. She stretched out facing the sky.

The night was clear and the moon seemed close enough to touch. Its light fell on the short pines and the mossy bald around her. The stars were millions of pinpricks of light in a blanket of darkness.

So much was behind her. So many memories and trials and miles. She'd made it into her fourteenth and final state, where September snowstorms weren't rare, where freezing temperatures could make even the heartiest mountain men call it quits and head for shelter. Maine was rugged. Maine was wild. In forty years, Maine would *still* have more uninhabited forest than any other continental state.

She couldn't have known it then, but much of America was pulling for her, clipping newspaper articles at kitchen tables and watching her traipse across the evening news on television, wondering whether she'd survive, this woman, in so mean a place. She carried their hopes along with her, but hers was a solitary walk—for peace, for serenity, for herself.

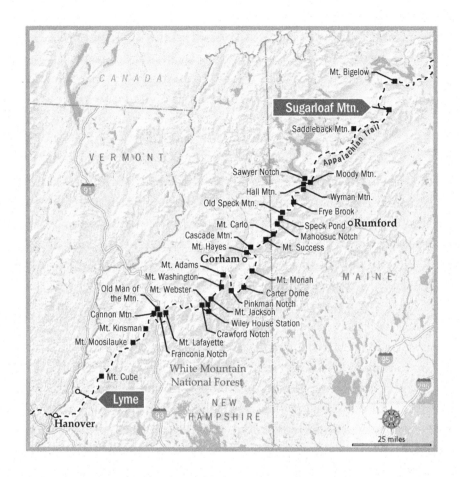

She stood that night, all alone, just 280 miles from that little brown sign atop Mount Katahdin, her chest full of crisp air and inspiration, her feet firm atop a forgettable mountain where the stars make you feel insignificant and important all at once.

And she sang.

— — — — —

In the late 1800s, just before Emma was born, an old man began walking clockwise on a nonstop 365-mile ovular route between the Connecticut and Hudson Rivers, a trip that took him precisely thirty-four days to complete. And then he did it again, and again— for more than thirty years. He was clothed entirely in leather. He had hand-made a suit, jacket, pants, and hat out of hide, and he came to be called "Old Leatherman." He slept in caves and natural shelters along his track where he kept gardens and stored food. Though he walked through dozens of towns, garnering enough attention after a few cycles that people set their watches by him, no one knew who he was. Although he was friendly enough to occasionally sit for a photograph, he didn't speak, and only once in a while grunted something low and unintelligible. Some thought he was French.

A myth developed about his origins, one that was never proven. The story had it that he was born Jules Bourglay, in Lyons, France, and that as a young man he had fallen in love with the daughter of a wealthy leather trader. He asked the merchant for his daughter's hand, and the merchant struck a deal: if Bourglay would work for him for a year, he would give his blessing to the marriage.

Bourglay agreed. But the business soon failed, due mostly to several of Bourglay's bad decisions. The wedding was off. Crushed, the young man went into hiding, then disappeared to the United States, where he set out on his continuous trip to walk his lover out of his mind, or assuage his guilt, or maybe none of that. Who is to know? Every eccentric needs a story, and if one is not provided, one will be created.

Despite Old Leatherman's mystique, Edward Payson Weston was probably America's most famous pedestrian. In 1860, he bet his friend that Abraham Lincoln wouldn't win the presidency. In 1861, he walked nearly five hundred miles, from Boston to Washington, DC, for Lincoln's inauguration, arriving a few hours late but in time to attend the inaugural ball. He launched his pro career a few years later, walking thirteen hundred miles from Portland,

Maine, to Chicago in twenty-six days. Two years later he walked five thousand miles for $25,000. Two years after that, the showman walked backward for two hundred miles. He competed in walking events against the best in Europe. Once, in his old age, he staged a New York to San Francisco one-hundred-day walk, but he arrived five days late. Peeved, he walked back to New York in seventy-six days. He told a reporter he wanted to become the "propagandist for pedestrianism," to impart the benefits of walking to the world. A devout pedestrian, he preached walking over driving. Unfortunately, he was seriously injured in 1927 when a taxicab crashed into him in New York, confining him in a wheelchair for the remainder of his life.

Weston wasn't the first long-distance walker who gained attention for his physical feats. Many came before him, including Lieutenant Halifax, who walked six hundred miles in twenty days. Foster Powell walked two hundred miles from London to York, England, and back in five days. In 1932, a man seen walking backward in Berlin turned out to be a Texan attempting to walk around the world backward wearing special glasses affixed with mirrors.

Later, in 1951, a New York couple claimed they had spent the previous twenty years walking city streets for a total of more than fifteen thousand miles. They said they had walked every single street of the five boroughs of New York City and had walked the varied boulevards of cities like Pittsburgh, Boston, Baltimore, and Denver. They became known as "America's Walkingest Couple."

The celebrated Captain Robert Barclay, a Scot, deliberately walked a mile in each of one thousand successive hours. The challenge took six weeks in 1809. If a normal human walks three to four miles per hour, then Barclay's attempt to walk just one mile per hour for one thousand hours stood apart for the sheer difficulty in pacing. Once every hour, he walked a mile, and stopped to rest.

Huge crowds came to watch, and journalists wrote of the event as though it were edge-of-your-seat entertainment.

Whether it was on a bet or to gain fame, to challenge oneself against nature or to pay amends for a lost love, those noted walkers—most all of them—had a purpose. In most cases, they let it be known. Mildred Lamb even wore a blue tunic that said PEACE PILGRIM on the front and 25,000 MILES ON FOOT FOR PEACE on the back. But the cases in which the motivations were held secret—as with Old Leatherman—observers, by nature, had to create a story to understand why one would set out on foot, leaving the shelters we build to plant us in civilization and set us apart from the world, the cars and houses and offices. To follow a path great distances, to open oneself to the world and a multitude of unexpected experiences, to voluntarily face the wrath of nature unprotected, was difficult to understand.

Emma Gatewood was coy when people asked why, at her age, she had decided to strike out on the long trail. As America's attention turned more toward Emma in her final days on the A.T., as newspaper reporters ramped up their dispatches to update the public on her condition and whereabouts, she offered an assortment of reasons about why she was walking. The kids were finally out of the house. She heard that no woman had yet thru-hiked in one direction. She liked nature. She thought it would be a lark.

I want to see what's on the other side of the hill, then what's beyond that, she told a reporter from Ohio.

Any one of the answers could stand on its own, but viewed collectively, the diversity of responses left her motivation open to interpretation, as though she wanted people to seek out their own conclusions, if there were any to be made. Maybe each answer was honest. Maybe she was trying to articulate that exploring the world was a good way to explore her own mind.

— — — — — —

On the morning of September 3, a man appeared on the mountain-side, east of the Maine state line. He was out of breath, and looked exhausted. Emma introduced herself. The huffing man asked how far away he was from the nearest lean-to, and she told him not too far. He said he was pooped from crawling through and climbing over rocks. He was carrying a large pack on his shoulders and he told Emma she was lucky hers was small.

She soon found out what he meant. Before her was Mahoosuc Notch, widely regarded as the most difficult mile on the Appalachian Trail. The narrow notch was hemmed in between two rocky mountain walls, clogged with cabin-sized boulders and gnarly root clusters, and speckled by deep caves. She climbed slowly, carefully, over and under the slippery, moss-covered boulders, and at times she had to lumber her pack through tight crevices and climb through behind it. It took two hours to make it out of the notch, and she was worn out by the time she got through, but still she continued on a few more miles.

She slept the night at the shelter by Speck Pond, the highest lake in Maine, and woke the next morning to cold rain, pattering at first, then turning to fat, freezing, percussive drops that would make sane people scramble for shelter. She had blown out another pair of shoes, the side of one and the toe of the other. She had mended them with some string, but they wouldn't hold much longer, and they did nothing to protect her feet from the wet or the biting cold. She wasn't near any town, so she had no choice but to deal with the misfortune.

She pushed over Old Speck Mountain, the state's third-highest peak and rough up and down, then through Grafton Notch and up Baldpate Mountain, which is topped by a slippery sheet of rock. Near the peak, at 3,662 feet, the cold rain turned to sleet, and she had to crawl on her hands and knees to keep from sliding off the face. To make matters worse, she was nearly blind. The only pair of glasses she could find had one lens, and it was fogged over. She cleared it constantly with her fingers or sleeve, but the world through one blind eye and one fog-tinted lens was an unusual and treacherous place. A misstep on much of the trail would've meant an injured ankle, but here on the sheer rock that was quickly accumulating ice, it could have meant plummeting to instant death. Or maybe that—instant death—would have been better than, say, winding up debilitated at the bottom of some hole, exposed to the elements, freezing or starving to death. She stepped carefully.

She came to a rock ledge about eight feet high, where she had to toss her sack to the ground below and climb down on a wet rope. She gripped it firmly, like she had held a thousand hoes, and slowly worked her way down. A little later, she arrived at a menacing crevice. The trail went straight across and, realizing she'd have to actually jump to the other side, she peered over the edge. Down in the pit, someone had painted a sign that read GO FAST. Emma tossed her sack across the gap and took a quick few steps on her bad knee and jumped, a great-grandmother aloft, then landed safely on the other side.

It was dark by the time she came upon an old shack near Frye Brook. The placed looked to be an abandoned sporting camp. It was nice and clean, so she climbed in through a broken window and made herself at home. She spread out old magazines on the floor and lay down atop the thin pallet of pictures and words, bundled against the cold night.

She walked across a paved mountain road the next day and noticed a man mowing along the shoulder on a tractor. Emma walked right up to him and introduced herself. He was Mr. Reed.

She asked him how far it was to the nearest town where she could buy a new pair of shoes. He looked down and noticed the strings holding hers together.

Six miles that way, he said, pointing, *or twenty miles that way.*

She didn't want to walk that far for shoes, even if the pair on her feet wouldn't last much longer. The two talked for a while, and Emma explained what she was doing. Mr. Reed told her he had a pair of sneakers at his house that he'd let her have, but he lived twenty miles away himself. Reed figured that if she could make it to the next road that intersected the trail by evening, he could have his wife meet her with the sneakers. Emma was grateful. She said good-bye and headed off, over Wyman Mountain and Hall Mountain, down through Sawyer Notch and up over Moody Mountain. When she appeared on the road, there sat Mr. Reed's wife and daughter. They'd gone into town and bought Emma a brand-new pair of white sneakers. Emma loosened the laces and began to slide in one foot, but the shoes were much too small. Somehow Mr. Reed had misunderstood and given his wife the wrong size.

Mrs. Reed apologized profusely and insisted Emma come to their home for the night. She said they'd bring her back to the trail in the morning, so Emma agreed. Mrs. Reed did Emma's laundry that night in their electric washing machine. The daughter called her friend, an avid hiker, and they made plans to accompany Emma the next day.

They made it back to the trail later than Emma would have liked on September 6, but she had enjoyed the company, and a warm place to sleep, so she didn't complain. The daughter and her friend set off with Emma, who was wearing new shoes, and took turns carrying her pack. They ate lunch at a shelter on Elephant Mountain, then hiked on, and though the trail was covered with blowdowns and obstacles, they all had an enjoyable day, putting in about ten miles.

Mrs. Reed met them to fetch the girls. She had brought a camera along and took pictures of the girls with Emma beside an Appalachian Trail sign. Emma walked on, alone, to Sabbath Day Pond, where she slept inside a lean-to, then shot across some hilly terrain to the Piazza Rock lean-to, then, on a knee that was really beginning to ache, she leaned into the tiresome, steep climb up Saddleback Mountain, 4,120 feet high. The cold wind blew through her layers of clothing, but she sat anyway to eat a snack on Saddleback and absorb the incredible view from the open crest. She saw on the dark horizon the Boundary Mountains, dividing the United States and Canada. She sensed a storm moving in, and as the sun fell the cold hung hard around her. She made it to a lean-to at Poplar Ridge and hunkered down against the bite. She didn't know what the stretch just ahead held for her, but it had been damning to previous hikers. Not long before, the entire section had been closed, marked with a sign that warned, TRAIL CLOSED, IN BAD CONDITION TO BIGELOW. TRAVEL AT YOUR OWN RISK. This had been the last remote stretch of trail to be completed on the entire A.T.

In fact, the trail through Maine almost ended before it was started. By 1933, construction and linkage of the trail was under way in most areas, but not northern New England. Some thought the trail should end at New Hampshire's Mount Washington because blazing the A.T. through Maine's rugged wilderness would make it difficult to access and maintain. After a two-year study, a proposed route for the trail appeared in a 1933 issue of *In the Maine Woods*, and Myron Avery began convincing volunteers and the Civilian Conservation Corps to help. They measured the trail, built campsites, and drew maps. However, much of their work was done hastily in an effort to extend the trail through to Katahdin.

In August 1937, the final section was completed on the north slope of Spaulding Mountain, but the problem of maintenance would persist. Through the 1940s, hurricane blowdowns and new logging operations caused the trail to fall into disrepair. Many of the trail volunteers were sent off to war, so it stayed in bad shape until the 1950s, when efforts to restore the path began anew.

Earl Shaffer, the first thru-hiker in 1948, experienced much of that difficulty. He wrote that the terrain in spots had been wrecked by a hurricane, with summer growth and brush pushing through fallen trees, and another stretch was "on corduroy," left from winter logging operations. Cross logs were suspended across the trail, on stumps and slash, and the snow had melted, leaving them exposed and rotting. "How hazardous this was can be imagined," he wrote.

And here came Emma, six years later, plodding along through stones and stumps, her knee getting worse with each footfall, up 4,250 feet of rock called Sugarloaf, past the ski lift, then down the other side and out onto the highway. There she met Mr. and Mrs. Richard Bell, who were spending a week at a friend's cabin and invited Emma to sit down for some breakfast. Her knee was throbbing and swollen. After breakfast, Richard Bell positioned Emma and his two young daughters by a trail sign and snapped their photograph before Emma cut away.

A fall storm was moving in as Emma hobbled on. She couldn't make it far. Her leg was hurting so badly. She stopped early, at Horns Pond, and ducked into a log shelter built by the Civilian Conservation Corps. It would have to do for the night. She couldn't walk any farther.

The next day was the same, only now she was fully limping, trying to keep weight off her knee. And the gray sky had opened, dumping rain on the wilderness, which was followed by a bitterly cold wind. She'd only made it a few miles, but Emma stopped at a shelter on Mount Bigelow to attempt to dry her things and thaw her fingers and toes. She tried to build a small fire near the shelter, but each time she made a little progress the strong gusts of wind blew most of the precious heat away. She tried again and again until she

. was frustrated. She gave up and was stomping out the few embers when a man walked up behind her. His presence startled her.

The man was the forest warden for the region, Mr. Vose, and he'd been looking for Emma. There was an item about her from the United Press in the newspaper:

FARMINGTON, Maine (UP)—A 67-year-old grandmother from Gallipolis, Ohio neared the end of a [2,050] mile hike on the Appalachian Trail today.

Mrs. Emma Gatewood, the hiker, is within 110 miles of her destination—Mt. Katahdin, Maine. She expects to reach the mountain in a fortnight.

Mrs. Gatewood, a sturdy five feet, four inches, started from Oglethorpe, Ga., on the Appalachian Trail last May 2. Mt. Katahdin is the end of the trail.

Mrs. Gatewood carries a light shoulder pack with a raincoat, blanket and enough food to last her between stop-overs. She walks only about eight miles a day now because of a lame leg.

Why the long walk?

Mrs. Gatewood, who has 11 children, 23 grandchildren, and two great-grandchildren, put it this way:

"After 20 years of hanging diapers and seeing my children grow up and go their own way, I decided to take a walk—one I always wanted to take."

The warden invited Emma to his cabin not far away. It was warm inside, and the fire felt good. She was happy to get out of the rain and cold, to have a chance to dry her belongings and give her knee a rest. There was still plenty of daylight left, but the warden advised Emma against going out on the trail again. The rain and cold were too much, and the stretch to the northeast was still damaged from a hurricane. He told her she couldn't get through the blowdown before nightfall.

She took his advice. He left the cabin to finish his shift, and while he was gone, Emma busied herself with chores. She washed the dishes, washed and dried her clothes, and fetched two buckets of spring water from a stream down the mountain a piece. She mopped the cabin floors and made biscuits and popped a skillet of popcorn over the dancing fire. The smell hit the warden when he came in from work. He was surprised and happy to see his place tidy and his supper made. He pulled a spare mattress from under his bed and made a pallet on the floor. The two strangers slept soundly to morning.

15

ALL BY MYSELF

It was hard to believe she'd come so far. A little more than one hundred miles left to Katahdin. She'd be doing just fine if her knee wasn't slowing her down, but things could be worse.

Emma started to climb Mount Bigelow about 8:00 AM, leaving the warden behind, and was approaching the fire tower on a patch of jagged rock when a raging gust of wind ripped over the bald, caught her, and tried to dislodge her from the mountain. She held firm, let the gale pass, and kept climbing.

She reached the stretch through which the hurricane had passed, and the toppled, tangled trees made hiking miserable. She struggled all day, climbing over splintered forest and corrupted stone. She found a used mattress at a shelter near Jerome Brook and made a bed for the night. A heavy frost set in the next day, and she wished she had something heavier to wear. She tried walking faster to keep warm, but the cold persisted. She stopped for breakfast the morning of September 14 at the West Carry Pond sporting camps. The proprietor, Adelaide Storey, gave Emma some snacks for the trail and took a few photographs. By now, Storey was used to ragged hikers schlepping through, as she'd met most of the thru-hikers who had come before and often housed the volunteers who worked on the trail.

Emma walked on to the East Carry Pond camps and rented a cabin. Franklin Gaskell ran the camps and his wife was out of town, so Emma cooked a biscuit supper for the man and his son. The next morning, Gaskell knocked on Emma's cabin door and told her she should join them for breakfast. He had a surprise.

She sat down at the table and he scraped several small fried trout onto her plate. The pond was thick with them. Emma had never eaten trout before and she loved the meal, devouring each one.

She followed a tote road past Pierce Pond and on a few more miles to the Kennebec River, arriving in the afternoon. There was no bridge across the swift-flowing, rocky stream. A forest warden, Bradford Pease, met her there with a canoe. He handed her a fat life preserver and she climbed aboard, bundled in a head scarf against the cold. Pease paddled Emma across the river to Caratunk, where a small crowd was waiting. Chief Warden Isaac Harris tugged the canoe onto the bank and greeted Emma. A reporter snapped her photograph as she climbed out of the canoe and stepped ashore, clutching her walking stick. She remembered then that she had dropped her raincoat on the far shore, so the warden started back across to fetch it.

Emma told the reporter she was determined to finish, but her pace had slowed from twelve miles a day to eight. "I'm having a little difficulty with my knee," she said. "Thought I'd rest overnight."

She learned from the reporter, an older woman herself, that the past few nights, including the night Emma had slept in the open shelter at Jerome Brook, the temperature had fallen well below freezing. Emma wasn't surprised. The nights had been bitterly cold. But walking and climbing in the mornings had thawed her.

"It didn't take me long to warm up," she said.

Her photograph ran on the AP wire and was reprinted in newspapers across the country with headlines such as HIKING GRANNY REACHES MAINE, HIKING GALLIPOLIS GRANDMA GETS REST NEAR GOAL, and OHIO GRANDMA NEARING END OF HIKE.

She walked to where the trail left the small town of Caratunk and then the reporter took her back to a large farmhouse called the Sterling Hotel for the night. Her clothes were wet again, so Emma asked the proprietor if she could dry them by the fire and kitchen stove. Emma made a skirt out of her blanket and spread the clothes out in the heat.

The next day was brutal as she approached the 100-Mile Wilderness. The trail was horrible with tangles of briers and swamp grass, made worse by the fact that she could barely see with only one lens in her glasses. She still walked hard and she had put in more than fifteen miles before she decided to quit for the day, but shelter was nowhere to be found. A campsite would have to do. The temperature had started to fall. Emma scrambled around collecting enough firewood to keep a flame burning all night. Her blanket and clothes did little to keep the warmth in or the hard cold out. She slept on the ground by the fire, rotating from side to side to keep warm, her breath rising like smoke. Fear kept her awake—not of bears or moose, but of catching herself on fire.

She rose early and walked ten miles by noon to the village of Blanchard, where an old man sold her breakfast for fifty cents, then she chipped off a few more miles to Monson, the last place to stock up on supplies before the 100-Mile Wilderness. She bought some groceries and tucked in at a motel kept by Sadie Drew in Monson. The walk through the forest was nice the next morning, though all the cabins at Bodfish Farm had been rented. One young couple let Emma stay with them. They served her supper and breakfast and didn't charge her for the night's sleep.

On September 19, her good fortune changed. The trail passed through a region of thick timber and several stretches were clogged with dense berry bushes. They snagged her dungarees and there was no clear path through. She could scarcely keep track of the

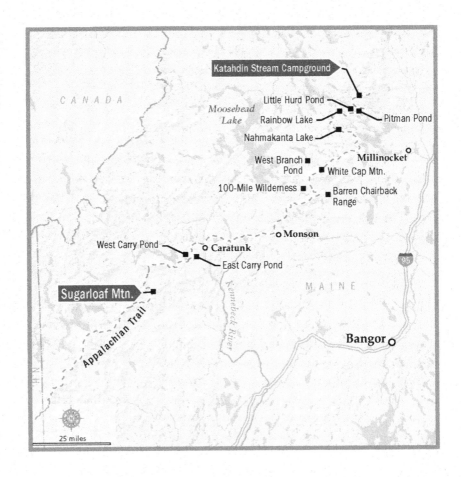

trail, much less blaze her way through the bushes. She climbed five peaks in the Barren Chairback Range, over rocks and around roots and through gullies and past the old stumps of white birches. Darkness had fallen by the time she walked into the Long Pond Camps, exhausted. A man showed Emma to her cabin and served her supper before she took a quick bath and fell asleep.

The tote road that carried her to White Cap Mountain was smooth, the walking easy if a bit chilly. From the top, on a clear day, Katahdin can be seen on the horizon, some seventy miles away. But once she got over the 3,654-foot peak, the hike grew miserable. There had been a forest fire. The trail blazes were few and far between. She had to wade through icy water for a section. There were no shelters in sight, so she walked two miles off the trail and got a nice cabin at the West Branch Pond Camps from Robert Tremblay, who owned the place. He brought her back to the trail the next morning and she again fought through a nightmarish and desolate patch of wilderness before stumbling upon the old shambles of a logging camp, which had been abandoned. Most of the buildings looked like they'd fall down with a decent push. She found the one that seemed the safest—or had a roof, at least. Inside, the floor was lined with long wooden benches, where she made a bed.

She fell the next day, coming down a hillside. It was not a fall that stopped her, but a fall bad enough to sprain her ankle, bruise her eye, and break her glasses, leaving her hobbling nearly blind for the last leg of the trail. She limped into Nahmakanta Lake, though, and hoped the dead red fox she found in front of the lean-to wasn't an omen that things would get worse. She got two long sticks and carried the carcass far into the woods. When she returned she cleaned the spot where it had been decomposing before bedding down for the night.

She hiked along the shoreline the next morning and stopped for lunch at the Nahamakanta Lake Camps, then walked blindly the last ten miles to Rainbow Lake, arriving around 4:30 PM. Katahdin jutted from the earth above the tree line on the opposite bank, and the sinking sun lit its peak. As Emma walked into camp, she recognized some of the men she'd met the year before. They were surprised to see her, after the experience last year, but they were ecstatic. They couldn't believe she'd come all the way from Georgia. One of the men washed Emma's clothes for her and she dried them on a line in Cabin 5, the same cabin she'd slept in on the last trip. She washed her long, gray hair and dried it, then sat down to supper of meat and vegetables with the men. They treated her like royalty.

Somehow, the place felt like home.

— — — — — —

P.C. was gone for good, and Emma was changing. Her children noticed that she was happier than they'd ever seen her. She had time to read more, time to garden, time to walk to visit friends, the freedom to travel.

"I am more than glad to be free of it all," she wrote in her diary. "Have been happy ever since."

Nelson graduated high school in 1941. The only social activity on Barkers Ridge was at the Baptist church, where they had fire-and-brimstone revivals in the summer. The boys, Nelson and Robert, would go to the revivals to try to convince pretty girls to let the boys walk them home. One night, Robert, in his early twenties, was sitting beside a girl and his whispers got a little loud.

A few days later, he and Nelson were on the farm, playing croquet shirtless and barefoot in the side yard, when a sheriff's deputy pulled up. He stepped out of the car and approached the boys and said he had a warrant from Robert's arrest. He said Robert had been disturbing the peace in church.

The boys stood there, white-faced, before Robert spoke up.

Well, let me go in the house and put on some clothes, he said. The deputy nodded and Robert walked inside.

Nelson talked to the deputy a while and collected the croquet set and put it in the garage, which had cracks between the wall slats. On his second trip in, he peered through the slats and saw Robert running down over the hill. He'd climbed out the back window.

Nelson didn't say anything to the deputy. They stood around a few more minutes.

It's taking him an awfully long time to put some clothes on, the deputy said. *Go on in there and check and see when he's going to be ready.*

Nelson followed his orders. He spent about five minutes inside and came back out.

Well, I went to every room in the house, and I can't find him, Nelson said. *Don't know where he is.*

Around midnight, Robert came back to the house.

Can I borrow your bike? he asked his younger brother. *I'm going to ride it to Monroe's.*

He left the bike in Gallipolis, at least thirty miles away. The next thing anybody heard, Robert was a soldier in the US Army.

Nelson went to work on a dairy farm in Mechanicsville, Ohio—labor so hard you could've wrung sweat out of his belt. When he turned eighteen, on December 28, 1941, he took a job with the telephone company and worked there a year before he, too, signed up for war. They put him on a train in Dayton, to Cincinnati, on to Fort Benjamin Harrison in Indiana, where he got shots and a haircut and even pulled KP duty before the sun had set on his first day as a soldier.

Before the war was over, Robert would be shot down over Munich and spend a year and a half in a German prisoner of war camp. People would whisper about how gaunt and pale he was when he came back to Ohio, a hero. Nelson, a paratrooper, would take a bullet to the thigh on Corregidor Island in the Philippines, recover, and get set to jump again when the war was called off.

"They were tough, that family," their cousin, Tommy Jones, would say years later. "Every last one of them."

As soon as Emma could, she sold the farm on Barkers Ridge and in 1944 moved back to Ohio, to Chesapeake, just across the river from Huntington, West Virginia. Louise went off to Marshall College while Lucy, the youngest, finished high school. Emma enrolled her in business school at Bliss College in Columbus, then bought a house in Rutland, Ohio, north of Gallipolis, on the Appalachian Plateau.

With nothing tying her down, Emma began to relocate frequently. She went to Pittsburgh and worked nine weeks, came back to Rutland to rent the house, then went to Dayton to work in a private boarding school for three months. In 1945, she moved back to Rutland and began renovating the home. She changed the cellar stairs, cut a doorway, installed banisters on the front porch, tore down an old fence, chopped down trees, demolished an old barn, and built a rock garden. Between projects she read and wrote poetry about nature, about God, about men, about tugboat landings and swimming holes and naughty birds and her new stage in life.

> My home I scrubbed and painted,
> Until I nearly fainted,
> Just for the lack of pelf,
> All by myself.

She self-published a collection that she distributed with great humility to friends and members of her family.

In 1949, Louise had a baby, Barbara, and needed help, so Emma moved back to Gallipolis. The next year, Emma and Louise bought a house together at 556 Fourth Avenue. They got along well. Emma read the newspaper every day and paid attention to local politics, often opining on the news—with sharp wit—in letters to the editor. On June 12, 1951, she sent this:

> Dear Editor: I was going to write and get in my three cents worth of opinion about how negligent the school board has been about making more room in our overfull schools, but decided not to disturb them in their lethargy.
>
> Instead I will give my version of what goes on with the peas in our gardens after they come up. I only have to say the rabbits ate my peas to get an argument started. Most everyone around here that has tried to raise peas say "the birds ate them off."
>
> My peas have vanished in the past quite a few times. One time when they were being eaten I put a chicken wire fence around the rows, and they were not bothered again. Anyone should know a fence will not keep out the birds. Another time when the peas were three or four inches tall they were eaten off clean, half way of the rows in a day or two. There happened to be a family of rabbits living in my garden at the time. Last year there were two rabbits lived in and around my garden and the peas were eaten. This year our garden is back of the athletic field fence and the holes were stopped to keep out the rabbits, which lived just on the other side. One could see them each morning out getting their breakfast, but the peas were not bothered.
>
> Someone will have to show me a bird eating peas before I will believe. There has been robins, starlings, English sparrows and other sparrows, the tanager, blue bird, doves, blackbirds, gold finches, cat birds, yellow hammers, wood thrush, and

indigo buntings, and not one of them have ever been seen to peek anything but bugs and worms in the garden.

Rabbits will also cut off the rose bushes as with a knife. I will venture to say that there are more rabbits in this town than in the same area in the country around. I do know that I can tramp the hills over and never see one rabbit, but see them here quite often. Build a good fence and raise peas or get rid of the rabbits and raise them.

—Emma Gatewood.

Louise got married in 1951, deeding her part of the house to her mother, and left Emma, for the first time in three decades, alone. All of her eleven children were on their own.

Emma would bounce around the next few years working menial jobs or caring for ailing relatives, to Pittsburgh, Pennsylvania, and Owensboro, Kentucky, and Miller, Ohio. But after Louise left, in 1951, Emma rented the house and went to work for five months at the county hospital in Columbus, where she likely first saw the *National Geographic* story about the Appalachian Trail, the one that promised the long path had been "planned for the enjoyment of anyone in normal good health" and "doesn't demand special skill or training to traverse" and gave the following scant advice to those considering a long hike:

Exercise caution over rough or steep parts.
Wear clothing suitable to the latitude, elevation, and time of year.
Plan where to pitch your tent, or find other shelter along the way.
Carry enough food, or know where meals may be had.

For an extended A.T. trip, thorough preparation should be
made. The condition of Trail stretches to be traversed
should be carefully checked.

Like the five reported thru-hikers before her and the thousands
who would follow, she hadn't been able to get the trail out of her
head. In July 1954, she flew to Maine and started south from the
summit of Mount Katahdin and got lost and very nearly couldn't
find her way out of the wilderness.

Go home, grandma, one of the rescuers had told her.

But she was back.

— — — — — —

The men told Emma to wait at Rainbow Lake so they could sum-
mon a warden to meet her at the west branch of the Penobscot River
to ferry her across. She waited around until 9:00 AM, then headed
east past Little Hurd Pond and Pitman Pond, walking about ten
miles before noon. When she got to the river, no one was there to
meet her. She climbed atop a large rock above the logging road to
sit and eat her lunch.

Two thousand miles west, in Denver, Colorado, unbeknownst
to most of the American public, President Dwight D. Eisenhower
was nearly dead. The former four-pack-a-day smoker, on vacation in
Denver, had played a round of golf the day before, then joined his
wife and doctor for dinner, where he complained of stomach pains,
which became worse as the evening turned to morning. The man
whose legacy would be the Interstate Highway System had suffered
a heart attack at the age of sixty-four, which would stick him on
the eighth floor of Fitzsimmons Army Hospital for seven weeks and
keep the nation on edge into the following year.

Back on the Appalachian Trail, the woman who had never had so much as a cold wasn't on her rock long before she saw dust plumes trailing two cars headed her direction.

The warden climbed out of one. Mary Snow from *Sports Illustrated* and Mrs. Dean Chase from the United Press in nearby Millinocket came out of the other. Emma looked worn out. Her eye was still bruised, but she seemed to be in good spirits. After the greetings, they climbed in the cars and drove a mile or so to a canoe launch. The warden pulled a boat off the top of his vehicle and slid it into the freezing water as the women talked. Mrs. Chase snapped a few photographs as Emma, the warden, and Mary Snow piled into the vessel and started for the other side. The warden had affixed a small motor on the boat and they were across in no time.

Mrs. Chase took the car around and was instructed to meet them at the campground near Katahdin. Emma and Mary Snow stepped ashore, thanked the warden, and began their hike together on a path alongside the Penobscot River. They talked as they walked. So much had happened since they had first met on Bear Mountain. Emma told her about the wind atop Mount Washington, about wading the hurricane-swollen creek with the navy boys, about having to push her sack through the holes in Mahoosuc Notch, about fashioning a discarded piece of rubber into an arch support. She told Snow about using a fork she found at a campsite to comb her hair. She told her about measuring distances between stepping stones in a swift-moving stream with her walking stick because of her broken glasses.

I couldn't see so good, Emma said.

Snow asked her where she had been sleeping.

Anywhere I could lay my bones, Emma said. Front porch swings. Picnic tables. Lean-tos. Logging camps.

What about animals? Snow asked.

Most people get scared when they come up against an animal, said Emma, *and right away think they have to make a fight out of it. Animals won't attack you unless you corner them. Fiddlesticks, I never even saw a bear. I made so much racket crashing and thumping through the woods.*

By the time the two arrived at York's sporting camps, it had begun to rain. Snow asked to use the telephone and called the Katahdin Stream Campground where Mrs. Chase was waiting, and asked Chase to come pick her up at York's camps. They talked some more while they waited.

Snow wondered about Emma's general impressions of the trail. Did it meet her expectations?

I read about this trail three years ago in a magazine and the article told about the beautiful trail, how well marked it was, that it was cleared out and that there were shelters at the end of a good day's hike, Emma said. *I thought it would be a nice lark. It wasn't. There were terrible blowdowns, burnt-over areas that were never re-marked, gravel and sand washouts, weeds and brush to your neck, and most of the shelters were blown down, burned down, or so filthy I chose to sleep out of doors. This is no trail. This is a nightmare. For some fool reason they always lead you right up over the biggest rock to the top of the biggest mountain they can find. I've seen every fire station between here and Georgia. Why, an Indian would die laughing his head off if he saw those trails. I would never have started this trip if I had known how tough it was, but I couldn't and wouldn't quit.*

When Mrs. Chase arrived, Emma said good-bye and walked the rest of the way to the Katahdin Stream Campground in the rain. She registered for a cabin. The warden built a fire in the stove for her and brought her a lamp. Mary Snow and Mrs. Chase arrived by car as the evening cold began to set in. The warden brought some extra blankets and the women talked a little more before Snow gave

Emma the balance of her lunch, and Snow and Chase climbed in the car and headed back to civilization in Millinocket.

Emma walked back to the warden's office and paid him for her cabin. On the walk back, she stopped at the different lean-tos, where fires lit the faces of campers, and chatted, telling her stories to the surprised and curious outdoorsmen. At the base of that mile-high mountain, on the 144th day of her journey, she felt important.

If the trail was a book, she was about to start the last chapter.

16

RETURN TO RAINBOW LAKE

SEPTEMBER 25, 2012

We woke in the dark at Katahdin Stream campground. I can't say woke, really, because it felt like I'd been awake all night, the kind of uncomfortable sleep that never fully sucks you in but instead keeps you right on the edge of consciousness. The pain was in my lower back, mostly, but it wouldn't be right to complain about spending a single night on the hard slats of a lean-to.

"Most people today are pantywaist," Emma Gatewood told a reporter five decades ago. I wonder what she'd think of us now. I wonder what she'd think of the gear we're packing by the light of our headlamps, into ergonomically designed backpacks with what must be hundreds of pockets. Our Leatherman tools and cook-stoves and iPhones with compass apps.

Our goal was to retrace Emma's steps up Katahdin, using her diary and old trail maps as our guide. I wanted to see what she saw, walk where she walked, in a maddening effort to better understand her by covering the same ground she did fifty-seven years before, to the day, on September 25, 1955. "The end of the trail," she wrote in her journal.

This was sacred ground.

Five months earlier, I stood on Mount Oglethorpe in Georgia with the same purpose. Like much of the trail, the start has shifted. The southern terminus is now at Springer Mountain—about twenty miles northwest of the more impressive Oglethorpe—where it was moved in 1958 because of development and farming. To try to get some sense of what Emma saw, I had to ignore several NO TRESPASSING signs on the mountaintop and cross private property before beginning a hike downhill. I'd tracked Emma's footfalls through Georgia, Pennsylvania, and Maryland, though the trail has changed so much that it was challenging to know exactly where she had walked. I had climbed the bluffs overlooking Harpers Ferry, West Virginia, where she stopped to enjoy the majestic view of the confluence of the Potomac and Shenandoah. I'd talked at length with her four surviving children—in Florida, Ohio, Arizona, and Arkansas—and her grandchildren, and I'd read her journals and many newspaper and magazine articles as well as a big box of correspondence her family has preserved. I had run my fingers over her old walking stick, a thin but sturdy branch from a wild fruit tree. I thought of climbing Katahdin, the highest point in Maine, as one last sacred pilgrimage, a search for the intangible.

In her book *Wanderlust: A History of Walking*, Rebecca Solnit writes:

> A path is a prior interpretation of the best way to traverse a landscape, and to follow a route is to accept an interpretation,

or to stalk your predecessors on it as scholars and trackers and pilgrims do. To walk the same way is to reiterate something deep; to move through the same space the same way is a means of becoming the same person, thinking the same thoughts.

The Katahdin ascent is much the same today as it was in 1955, but more than half of the trail in Maine had been relocated. In 1968, after the passage of the National Trails System Act, the Maine Appalachian Trail Club reviewed the entire trail in the state and began to move the A.T. to a route that was more rewarding for the hiker and could be better maintained. Major relocation projects ran from the mid-1970s to the late '80s.

To be certain our climb was historically accurate, my wife and I hired Paul Sannicandro as a guide. Paul, a good-natured outdoorsman, is the trail supervisor at Baxter State Park, responsible for maintaining some 225 miles of footpath through a two-hundred-thousand-acre wilderness with forty-seven mountain peaks and sixty-seven lakes and ponds. The park was a gift to the people of Maine from former governor Percival Baxter, who bought and donated most of the land over three decades and established a fund, with his own millions, for its maintenance and operation. He wanted the park to remain wild, and despite logging and hunting and thousands of visitors a year, it has maintained for the most part the feeling and spirit of wilderness.

We had met Paul two days before, over Maine lobsters at a dive in Millinocket. He reviewed our itinerary and he checked our packs to be sure we'd brought the appropriate clothing for the cold weather. I was already feeling like a pantywaist.

Using Emma's journal, Paul had calculated that she would have crossed the West Branch of the Penobscot near Abol Bridge, then walked along the northern bank of the Penobscot a few miles to the intersection of Nesowadnehunk Stream, then to Katahdin Stream Campground, where she spent the night before a hike up the Hunt Trail, past Thoreau Spring, to Baxter Peak. The next day, we followed her path, putting in about nine easy miles before we reached camp at the base of Katahdin, where we found a plaque implanted into a boulder:

> MAN IS BORN TO DIE. HIS WORKS ARE SHORT LIVED.
> BUILDINGS CRUMBLE, MONUMENTS DECAY, WEALTH VANISHES.
> BUT KATAHDIN IN ALL ITS GLORY FOREVER SHALL REMAIN
> THE MOUNTAIN OF THE PEOPLE OF MAINE
>
> P.P.B.

The next morning, we filled our canteens with cold water from the stream, finished stuffing our backpacks, and dropped our extra supplies at the ranger station. It was nearly freezing and still dark when we signed the register and left the campground at 5:50 AM, the same time Emma left, with guide Paul leading the way through the moonlit forest, flanked on both sides by aspens and maples, evergreens and ferns. Six hikers had left before us and many more would follow. I tried to imagine Emma traversing the rough terrain in the dark, her only light coming from a small flashlight. Enough day-hikers come through this stretch now that the path is eight feet wide in places, but in 1955 it wasn't much more than a game trail.

It would have been impossible to accurately recreate in this spatial theater Emma's misfortune. Her bad knee. Her broken glasses and busted shoes. The fatigue she must have felt after climbing mountains for 144 straight days on sixty-seven-year-old legs. But I soon found a thin walking stick, our common denominator, and let those other thoughts percolate with each step. Katahdin was dry for our hike, but it had rained in the days preceding Emma's, so the flora was still wet then. Her shoes and dungarees were soaked quickly. "And I was not very warm," she wrote. Besides the dungarees and long-sleeved button-up she was wearing, she brought along every scrap of clothing she found in her bag. A T-shirt, a men's heavy wool pullover sweater, a satin-lined wool jacket, and a raincoat.

The trail runs through spruce thickets alongside Katahdin Stream, past a three-tiered waterfall that sounds like applause. It's barely visible in the gray light of morning as we pass, but I try to imagine Emma here, her ribs rising and falling with each heavy breath, trying to balance her sack on her shoulder while struggling over land where it appeared the sky had rained rocks. Alone.

A century before she came through, before Earl Shaffer and Benton MacKaye, another pilgrim climbed this mountain. It was September 1846, and a group of men passed through Millinocket, then poled and paddled up the west branch of the Penobscot, camping at Abol Stream before moving up the flanks of Katahdin, or, as Henry David Thoreau called it, Ktaadn. Thoreau took the lead, bushwhacking through the backcountry, until he had a clear view of the mountain, which was different from any he'd ever seen due to the large proportion of naked rock rising above the forest. His companions set up camp, but Thoreau seized the remaining light and attempted to summit, climbing through "the most treacherous and porous country I ever traveled," stopping at the skirt of a cloud. He notes that before him, Ktaadn, an Indian word meaning highest land, was first ascended by white men in 1804, and only a handful had climbed it in the intervening forty-two years. "Besides these," he writes, "very few, even among backwoodsmen and hunters, have ever climbed it, and it will be a long time before the tide of fashionable travel sets that way."

Thoreau turned back that day, but ascended again the following morning, leaving his companions far behind. He reached the tableland, a bare, rocky, gently sloping plateau, which he calls an "undone extremity of the globe." He seems to have felt out of place on the mountaintop, frightened to be there.

"This ground is not prepared for you," he writes.

Is it not enough that I smile in the valleys? I have never made this soil for thy feet, this air for thy breathing, these rocks for thy neighbors. I cannot pity nor fondle thee here, but forever relentlessly drive thee hence to where I *am* kind. Why seek me where I have not called thee, and then complain because you find me but a stepmother? Shouldst thou freeze or starve, or shudder thy life away, here is no shrine, nor altar, nor any access to my ear.

On his descent, he practically comes apart.

It is difficult to conceive of a region uninhabited by man. We habitually presume his presence and influence everywhere. And yet we have not seen pure Nature, unless we have seen her thus vast, and drear, and inhuman, though in the midst of cities. Nature was here something savage and awful, though beautiful. I looked with awe at the ground I trod on, to see what the Powers had made there, the form and fashion and material of their work. This was that Earth of which we have heard, made out of Chaos and Old Night. Here was no man's garden, but the unhandselled globe. It was not lawn, nor pasture, nor mead, nor woodland, nor lea, nor arable, nor waste-land. It was the fresh and natural surface of the planet Earth. . . . There was there felt the presence of a force not bound to be kind to man. It was a place for heathenism and superstitious rites,—to be inhabited by men nearer of kin to the rocks and to wild animals than we.

I'm not sure if Emma ever read Thoreau's essay on Katahdin, but her own words hint often at the idea that she was measuring herself against nature, that the wild brought her context like a gift.

On the trail, she said, "the petty entanglements of life are brushed aside like cobwebs." Thoreau writes that "some part of the beholder, even some vital part, seems to escape through the loose grating of his ribs as he ascends. He is more lone than you can imagine."

Emma told a reporter that she had found "an aloneness more complete than ever." I've thought a lot about that statement. Larry Luxenberg, who interviewed some two hundred A.T. hikers for his book *Walking the Appalachian Trail*, says that if you applied the Myers-Briggs personality type indicator to the more than eleven thousand thru-hikers since Earl Shaffer, you'd find that the vast majority were introverts. Not so for Emma, who had no problem introducing herself to strangers or asking for a place to spend the night. She enjoyed company, to be sure, but found an equal reward in solitude.

An hour or so into our hike we came to a bare spot in the trees. The sun was rising in the east, stretching bars of purple and pink across the horizon, beyond the treetops. After a slog up the mountain—and I mean to lend emphasis to the word *up*; I ran a marathon in four hours in March, but I was breathing heavily and my legs trembled if I stood still for any length of time—we broke through the timberline and found ourselves facing a ridge of bare boulders known as Hunt Spur.

Our guide was well versed when it came to safety, and he had recounted for us several harrowing mountain rescues in which he had taken part. Anecdotally, injury visited hikers of all ages and skill levels. He told us about a man who tried to brace himself between two large boulders, and his own body weight had injured both shoulders. He had to be strapped to a stretcher and passed, rescuer by rescuer, down the mountain.

When we were exposed on that bare ground, the temperature seemed to plummet. The wind bit hard. Paul reminded us that we wanted to add and remove layers to avoid perspiring, a key to cold-weather survival.

"When I got above the timberline, the wind nearly blew me off," Emma wrote. "I started putting on my extra clothes, a tee shirt, a man's heavy wool slip-on sweater, a satin lined wood jacket, and raincoat. By the time I was at the top with two pairs of wool socks, and gloves with raincoat sleeves over them, wool hood, silk scarf and plastic rainhood on my head, and I was just comfortable."

At several spots, metal bars have been buried into bald boulders. Hikers must climb using the rods, like climbing on top of monkey bars. Somewhere along the spur, my wife, Jennifer, winced in pain.

"You twisted your ankle?" I asked.

"Yeah," she said, favoring her right foot. "A little."

She promised she was OK, perhaps out of stubbornness, and hiked on. But it was noticeably causing her pain. Paul insisted we stop, so we did, behind a boulder that shielded us from the strong wind. Jennifer was hiking in five-toed Vibrams, but we'd brought along a pair of lace-up desert boots we bought at an Army-Navy surplus store. As Paul examined her ankle, it struck me that even a minor injury could be a major problem at this height. We'd been hiking nearly four hours, still an hour or so short of Baxter Peak. Getting back down on a broken ankle would be damn near impossible. I pictured a helicopter hovering above the ridge, trying to hold steady, lowering a basket to carry Jennifer to safety. I wondered what Emma would have done. We had cell phones, and we'd already seen a dozen or so day-hikers, but she found the mountain empty.

Paul thought Jennifer should change into the boots for more ankle support, and she begrudgingly laced them up, breathing warmth onto her bare fingers so she could feel the laces. We had a drink of water and ate some nuts and energy bars before setting off again, carefully. The surroundings, from our vantage point, were enough to steal your breath. The sun was finally high enough to catch the dozens of lakes and ponds far below, painting them white, as if someone had dropped a giant mirror on Katahdin and the shattered shards lay splayed beneath us.

It was hard to identify any human activity at all in what must be the largest contiguous block of undeveloped, minimally maintained land in New England. I remembered something I'd read about Emma's climb in 1954, the first time she'd ever been on top of a mountain. She put on a black wool sweater at the top and ate a lunch of raisins while she counted the lakes and ponds below. She gave up when she got to one hundred.

We reached the Gateway, where the terrain levels off before rising again to the peak. Much of the tableland was covered with short, intricate, beautiful vegetation called diapensia. It's a minimalist plant that looks like an evergreen pincushion, no more than three or four inches tall. Its tiny leaves grow tightly together, insulating the plant's interior from cold. Intermingled with the diapensia is Bigelow's sedge, a rare flowering plant that grows on flatlands at high alpine elevations. Both plants are threatened and must be monitored carefully, Paul tells us. If alpine regions shrink because of global warming or human activity, there may be no suitable habitat left for Bigelow's sedge. And the Katahdin Arctic butterfly would disappear with it.

The small butterfly is a subspecies of Polixenes Arctic and it is found nowhere else in the world besides the one thousand acres of tablelands on Mount Katahdin. Scientists have not accurately measured the population, but they do know it fluctuates dramatically. The females lay their eggs on sedges, and when the eggs hatch the larvae feed on the plants and slowly mature. In winter the larvae hibernate before starting to eat again in the spring. They mature to pupae in late summer and finally emerge the following year as adults, only to fly around for about a month, completing the two-year life cycle.

Park rangers here at Baxter were shocked when, in the mid 1990s, federal agents raided the homes of a pest exterminator and two businessmen in California and Arizona and found thirty-seven Katahdin Arctic butterflies among a collection of twenty-two hundred rare insects. Their audacious poaching operation—agents found letters from one man advising the others to, if caught, say, "Sorry, I didn't know you couldn't catch butterflies here"—sparked the first federal case against butterfly poaching and opened rangers' eyes to the threat of commercial butterfly collecting. What's interesting is that the Katahdin Arctic isn't big and beautiful like the monarch or the morpho. The prized and valuable butterfly is small, and dull brown in color. This target for poachers looks like a moth.

A more predictable, manageable threat to Mount Katahdin habitats is walking. Hikers have destroyed diapensia and sedge through the years by trampling, until the park established a well-marked trail and signs to keep people off the plants. It's soon clear that not all hikers bother to read them, and traipse across the tableland off the path. Paul, pissed off, shouts a stern warning to an oblivious hiker who is marching through the delicate flora.

"Sorry, man," the hiker says.

Knowing the tenuous nature of plants and insects this high up makes me wonder if we should even be here. I left camp thinking we'd be trying to find Thoreau's sacred ground, Emma Gatewood's sacred ground, but I was beginning to feel like an interloper—even if we were sticking to the center of the trail.

Thoreau Spring, in the middle of the tablelands, looked like a mud puddle, swarmed by the dozens of boot prints from yesterday's hikers. As we would soon learn, there was a good chance that some of those footprints were left by men and women who had been inspired by Emma Gatewood's journey here. But what had inspired her?

We took a short break by the mountaintop spring and I watched it slowly trickle downhill. A thought struck me: Climbing a mountain, climbing this mountain, means following a river against the flow through the valley, then a stream up on the mountain's flank, past waterfalls, and, eventually, to this little spring. It means walking against the hydrological cycle, against the order of things, to the source of life. To youth. To birth.

Back home, I had told a friend, a newspaper guy out in Wichita, Kansas, what I had been trying to do, how I'd been stalking Grandma Gatewood on the Appalachian Trail, trying to get inside her head. My friend shared a story.

In 1982, he and his wife put on their packs and began a multiday hike up Pikes Peak in Colorado. After three or four days, when they'd finally reached the timberline, they were both exhausted. The flatlanders were in no shape to climb the 14,115-foot mountain. Every breath burned. Then my friend saw a bronze plaque affixed to a boulder, a memorial to a death on the mountain in 1957.

DEDICATED TO THE MEMORY OF
G. INESTINE B. ROBERTS
AGE 88 YEARS
WHO DIED AT TIMBERLINE
AFTER HER FOURTEENTH ASCENT
OF PIKES PEAK

Thirty years later, my friend still remembered the marker. He remembered being amazed that this octogenarian returned to the peak time and again, and met death on her final descent.

"What is it with old people and mountains?" he asked.

That's a fine question.

— —— —— —— —— —

At Katahdin's summit, we found a surprise.

Several hikers had passed us on the climb, but we never expected to find a crowd. There were perhaps thirty-five hikers at the summit, and most of them were thru-hikers who had reached their final destination. Young and old and bearded and smelly. A group of them who had met and become friends on their long journey were cracking Budweisers and passing a joint. They had affixed a video recorder to the end of a walking stick and they were filming themselves, digital memories of the end of their nature hike. They spoke in a sort of trail code, which lent the scene a certain exclusivity, like a party you could get into only if you knew the secret knock. A young man with a big red bushy beard climbed atop the wooden KATAHDIN sign and balanced in a crow yoga pose as the rest of them laughed. There were at least two marriage proposals. Both couples had first met on the trail.

In 2012, Appalachian Trail Conservancy records show, twenty-five hundred thru-hikers started in Georgia. Fewer than half— 1,012—logged in at Harpers Ferry, the psychological halfway point. One in five reported making it to Mount Katahdin. I sat on a rock and watched as even more pilgrims made their way to the sign. Their euphoria was contagious and almost moved me to tears. A gray-haired couple, slower and calmer than the rest, touched the sign and then embraced. They were both crying.

"You know it has to be this hard," the woman said. "It has to be."

Even though the A.T. has become better maintained and more crowded over the years, finishing a thru-hike remains a remarkable achievement. More than eleven thousand people have hiked all two-thousand-plus miles, many in sections. But among thru-hikers, on average, three out of four who start never finish, according to the Appalachian Trail Conservancy. The number of two-thousand-milers, as they're called, has been on the rise in recent years, growing from 562 in 2005 to 704 in 2011.

Those numbers would have seemed preposterous to the trail's planners and early organizers. In the 1930s, just five people reported hiking the entire trail, all of them in sections. (The trail was completed in 1937.) Only three finished in the 1940s—Earl Shaffer was the lone thru-hiker—a period during which the trail was again incomplete or unconnected in places. In the 1950s, when Emma came along, just fourteen reported two-thousand-mile hikes.

Then the numbers started to climb. The number of completions more than doubled in the 1960s: thirty-seven people logged in. Nearly eight hundred hiked all the way in the 1970s. The 1980s saw 1,420 completions. The 1990s: 3,301. The 2000s: 5,876.

Among the ranks of two-thousand-milers are two six-year-old boys, an eighty-one-year-old man, an eighty-year-old woman, a blind man, barefoot sisters, a cat, and a woman who, in 2011, reportedly completed the entire trail in forty-six days, eleven hours, and twenty minutes, the fastest-ever unofficial time.

And as peaceful as it may seem, thru-hiking the Appalachian Trail can drip with controversy. It started with the legend himself: Earl Shaffer. The A.T.C. was skeptical of his claim until he showed hundreds of slides and gave a vast description of his trip. Over the years, Shaffer became the skeptic, writing of his suspicions that other early thru-hikers, including Grandma Gatewood, may have taken shortcuts.

In the mid-1990s, an elderly gentleman named Max Gordon told the *Appalachian Trailway News* that he and five other teenage Boy Scouts from the Bronx had thru-hiked the trail in 1936, which, if true, would have made Earl Shaffer the seventh thru-hiker instead of the first. The man had solid recall of certain experiences along the trail, but other sections were blurry gaps in his memory. He could remember the names of just two of the other Scouts, and both were dead. He told the publication that he never knew the hike was important until he received a mailer from the A.T.C. in his old age and decided to bring it to someone's attention.

Even without supporting evidence, the Appalachian Long Distance Hikers Association in 2000 adjusted its list of the first two-thousand-milers, and Earl Shaffer called for a reexamination. However, it was Shaffer's record that was again called into question, in 2011. A West Virginia lawyer and backpacker named Jim McNeely had been poring through Shaffer's old notebook, which had been turned over to the Smithsonian Institution upon Shaffer's death in 2002. The lawyer was trying to piece together the path of the old A.T., as it was in Shaffer's day, when he discovered that Shaffer had bypassed 170 miles of trail, taking shortcuts, accepting rides in cars, and walking on roads. McNeely, a former prosecutor, published an unbelievably detailed, nineteen-chapter, 164-page report that painted Shaffer as a fraud and hypocrite.

Presented with solid evidence that Shaffer had at least misrepresented his hike in revisions, the A.T.C. and the Appalachian Trail Museum took an interesting stance. Basically, *We're not in the detective business.* Shaffer's place in history stands as the first *reported* thru-hike.

The hiking community went nuts, dividing into two camps: the "purists" or "whiteblazers," who believe you must walk by every single white blaze—and if you miss one, you return to where you missed it; and the "hike your own hike" group, which tends to be less austere about rules on a spiritual walk from Georgia to Maine.

The two sides could argue for days about what constitutes a thru-hike, which is testament, ultimately, to their love for the trail, their love for this experience.

— — — — — —

The joy at the top of Katahdin was palpable, for good reason. It felt wrong for me to intrude on their blissful and sacred moment, but I awkwardly approached the group and asked if they were familiar with Grandma Gatewood. They all nodded.

"Gotta have respect for someone who hiked the trail barefoot," a man said.

I didn't correct him. Her legend had evidently blossomed. I had heard some wild tales as well, growing up, from my mother. One has Emma scaring away a black bear with an umbrella.

Atop the mountain that day, I didn't talk to a single person who wasn't at least vaguely aware of Emma's accomplishments. What's more, many of them had been inspired by her, all these years later.

"When it got hard, I'd think about her," one of the hikers said. "I'd think, 'She did it. I can, too.' "

— — — — — —

Emma Gatewood reached the summit at Baxter Peak without ceremony before noon on September 25, 1955, twenty-six days before her sixty-eighth birthday, having hiked 2,050 miles through thirteen states, from Mount Oglethorpe in Georgia to the highest point on Mount Katahdin in Maine, the spot where the very first rays of morning sunshine touch the United States.

She planted her seventh pair of tennis shoes on the rocky top of the precipice, alone. Physically, even in her bulky red mackinaw, she was a shadow of the woman who had started walking 146 days before. She had lost thirty pounds. Her glasses were broken; her knee was sore. She wore the clothes of an immigrant to her altar in the sky and spoke aloud to an invisible audience.

I did it, she said. *I said I'd do it and I've done it.*

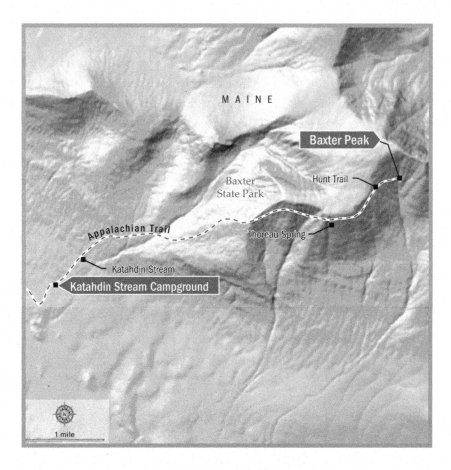

The sign planted in a rock cairn at the top said:

KATAHDIN
NORTHERN TERMINUS OF
THE APPALACHIAN TRAIL,
A MOUNTAIN FOOTPATH
EXTENDING 2050 MILES TO
MT. OGLETHORPE, GEORGIA

As the wind beat against her cheeks, Emma sang the first verse of "America the Beautiful," words that had come to a different woman in 1893, as she looked down from Pikes Peak.

O beautiful for spacious skies,
For amber waves of grain,
For purple mountain majesties
Above the fruited plain!

A storm began moving onto the mountain and she didn't want to be trapped. She began to sign the register when a gust of wind caught her and nearly blew her down. She regained her balance. Then the sun peeked through the clouds for just a moment, like a wink, as though the heavens were acknowledging her presence.

17

ALONENESS MORE COMPLETE THAN EVER

She was a portrait of proper. Her iron-gray hair was clean and combed and pulled back. She wore a soft white blouse, red rayon suit, and medium-heeled black shoes.

"I decided to look a bit more presentable on the way back," Emma told Mrs. Dean Chase, the reporter with the United Press. "You know, it feels kind of good to get back into civilized clothes."

She was the talk of the country. The headlines ran in newspapers everywhere.

Mrs. Gatewood Completes Hike
Grandma Plans New York Visit as Hike Ends
GRANNY TIRED

Earl Shaffer's hike had prompted a few newspaper stories and the article in the *National Geographic* that inspired Emma. Gene Espy's hike a year later made local papers. The attention Emma received was unprecedented.

"A jovial little grandmother who lost 30 pounds in her trek along the Appalachian Trail said today that she has had 'all the walking I've wanted for a long time,'" read a story in the *Baltimore Sun*. "New Hampshire, she said, was the toughest part of the journey. Maine offered a few serious obstacles where there were 'blow-downs' of trees along the trail. Several times Mrs. Gatewood fell and strained an ankle or knee, slowing her. There has been frost every morning of the last week but Mrs. Gatewood said she found shelter and at least one good meal daily at sportsmen's camps. There is a little snow on the mountain."

She was called "sprightly," "robust," "doughty," "determined," "straight-laced and old-fashioned," "strong," "frail-looking," and, surprisingly, "tall." According to the journalists, she reported feeling in "tip-top shape" and ready to walk "another thousand miles." She was in a good mood, she said, because this was the first morning that she "didn't get up at 6 o'clock and have to climb a mountain." She calculated that she had spent about two hundred dollars on the trail, roughly ten cents a mile.

She sent her glasses with Mary Snow to have them fixed and fitted with new lenses. The president of the Millinocket Chamber of Commerce gave her a tour of the nearby paper mill and treated her to lunch at the Great Northern Hotel. That afternoon, he drove her back to the chamber, where a group of businessmen and dignitaries had gathered. They presented Emma with a large picture of Mount Katahdin.

She posed for photographs in a potato field and fetched her repaired glasses from the ophthalmologist and ate a steak dinner with Mary Snow on the train to Bangor, courtesy of the Bangor and

Aroostook Railroad, where she scratched out a postcard, addressed it to a Roman Catholic parish in Harlem and dropped it in the mail, still unaware that she'd stayed the night with the leaders of two rival street gangs.

"I made it!" she wrote. "Remember me to all those young men I owe my life to. Please tell them they are welcome to come visit me anytime, as also are you. Love, Emma."

Over the next few days, Mary Snow gave Emma a tour of New York City, of the Empire State Building, Chinatown, and the wharf, as swarms of urbanites buzzed around them. It was a city she had only known before through the newspaper columns of Gallipolis's native son O. O. McIntyre. He called his daily dispatch "the letter," and his stories often had the feel of a postcard to the folks back home. He wrote of the telescope man on the curb, the Bowery lodging houses, the drifters, chorus girls, gunmen, the speakeasies on side streets, fake jewelry auction sales, chop houses, antique shops, cafeterias. Now Emma took it all in with her own eyes.

When it was time for her to go, Snow drove her to LaGuardia Airport and put her on a plane for home. She was carrying her walking stick, as always, and as she boarded the plane, the other passengers and crew kept trying to assist her, as if she were crippled.

Going back to the rolling hills of southern Ohio was like a victory tour, as Emma visited family, received phone calls from well-wishing friends, met her seven-month-old great-grandchild for the first time, and gave interviews to the reporters who had learned of her return. She said the people she had met along the trail were "extry nice"—all but the snooty woman who turned her away and the boy who called her a lady tramp.

"I thought it would be fun to walk the trail but I soon found that it was anything but that," she told one reporter. She explained how she had blown through seven pairs of shoes—four cloth-topped, two made of leather, the last a pair of sneakers—and used a total of five rolls of adhesive tape, mostly for ankle support. She mentioned how bad the bugs were and explained how she had fixed sassafras leaves in the band of her sunshade, dangling over her ears, to keep the pests off.

"I didn't get started sooner," she said, "because when you're raising a family of 11, you can't just run off when you want to. . . . I got to the point where I had time, and I decided, 'That'll be a nice lark for me.'"

When a reporter from Baltimore called her a celebrity, she responded: "I wish you people'd stop calling me names."

Was she afraid?

"If I'd been afraid," she said, "I never would have started out in the first place."

It was as though she was made for the moment.

"I slept wherever I could pile down," she told the local paper. "Course, sometimes they weren't the most desirable places in the world, but I always managed. A pile of leaves makes a fine bed, and if you're tired enough, mountain tops, abandoned sheds, porches, and overturned boats can be tolerated. I even had a sleeping companion. A porcupine tried to curl up next to me one night while I slept on a cabin floor. I decided there wasn't room for both of us.

"Though there were a lot of times I had to parcel out my food to make it last, I didn't have to break any laws to get it. And when it didn't last—well, I've eaten many a wild berry and chewed on many a sassafras, wintergreen, peppermint, and spearmint leaf.

"What the Lord didn't provide, I did. One day I was walking down the road and came upon a tin can. I turned it over a couple times with the tip of my cane and found a full, unopened can of beef stew. Opened it with my knife, and dined real well that night."

She said the trip was the most valuable summer of her life.

"It took me a long time to get to the top," she said, "and when I did and signed my named on the register, I never felt so alone in my life."

— — — — — —

The grown-up Gatewood children were alarmingly unsurprised that their mother had spent nearly five months in the woods, with rattle-snakes and street gangs, on a mile-high mountain with a sprained ankle and broken glasses. Maybe it's their stock.

"We didn't worry about her because she always took care of herself," Lucy told me, "and she taught us to take care of ourselves."

"I didn't know where she was or what she was doing," said Nelson, "and that was normal."

"Some people say, 'Weren't you worried?'" said Louise. "I said, 'No, we weren't worried.' She knew what she was doing. And if that's what she wanted to do, more power to her."

"She was just a normal person," said Nelson. "Nothing extra."

"We didn't know that she had become a kind of celebrity until later," said Rowena.

"When she came off the trail, she called from Huntington, West Virginia," said Charles Gatewood, Monroe's son and Emma's grandson. "She said, 'Come get me.' Dad said, 'You've walked all that way, surely you could walk the rest of the way to Gallipolis.'"

"You know, it wasn't that impressive to me, when she walked the Appalachian Trail the first time," said their cousin, Tommy Jones, who still lives in the family's old homestead on the Ohio River. "I think she was sixty-seven, right? Well, I knew how strong she was physically, and how she liked outdoors living. So for her, I didn't think that was anything exceptional."

Maybe she didn't either.

— — — — — —

Her celebrity rising, Emma was quickly summoned back to New York to appear on NBC's *Today* with Dave Garroway, where she was the featured guest. She walked in range of the cameras from a side door, wearing blue jeans, a checkered jacket, and tennis shoes, and she carried her old sack. In place of her eyeshade she wore a dark beret. She told Garroway and a nationwide audience that she could have walked another thousand miles beyond Katahdin "if necessary." Garroway asked her why she made the long walk. She said she had always strolled through the hills for pleasure, and when she read the roseate magazine story, she just decided she'd try it.

Afterward, she went to the Empire Hotel to try out for *Welcome Travelers*, a confessional quiz show hosted by "Smilin'" Jack Smith. She earned a spot and they filmed the show the following morning, after several rehearsals. Emma won two hundred dollars—exactly what she spent on the trail. She caught a ride on a sightseeing bus around New York and stopped at an antique shop to buy Mrs. Dean Chase of Millinocket a brass ashtray in the shape of a shoe.

Her next stop was Pittsburgh to visit her daughters, Rowena and Esther. She had barely touched down when the newspapers started calling. A reporter for the *Pittsburgh Press* asked her about her plans for the future.

"That's a secret," she said. "But if I go for another hike I'll let my family know like I did the last time—with postcards."

She told them all the same thing. "Nobody," she said, "is going to get out of me what's going through my head on that score."

She wouldn't say so, but she was already thinking about the trail again.

— — — — —

On June 25, 1956, in Washington, DC, the US House of Representatives convened to handle a slate of important business, including the scheduling of a discussion of a postal rate increase and to amend the Federal Property and Administrative Services Act of 1949. Ohio

Rep. Thomas A. Jenkins, a Republican from Ironton, addressed Democratic Speaker of the House John William McCormack.

"Mr. Speaker, I ask unanimous consent to extend my remarks at this point in the record," he said.

"Is there objection to the request of the gentleman from Ohio?" McCormack asked. There wasn't.

"Mr. Speaker," Jenkins began,

Mrs. Emma Gatewood, a resident of Gallipolis, Ohio, in our congressional district, won for herself national fame a few months ago. In spite of the fact that she was 67 years old and a great-grandmother, she hiked by herself 2,050 miles over rugged mountainous course. She hiked the rough and rugged Appalachian Trail from Fort Oglethorpe, Ga., to the summit of mile-high Mount Katahdin in wild and rugged northeastern Maine.

In performing this great undertaking, she wore out seven pairs of shoes. She carried only a blanket and a small supply of rations. She reached this wild and rugged goal after walking for 146 days. She averaged 17 miles a day and lost 24 pounds of weight. Her accomplishment brought forth many comments from mountain people. One old and experienced Maine woodsman said of her, "We have got to hand it to her. It takes guts, pioneer guts, to do that kind of a job."

Mrs. Gatewood read about the trail 3 years ago—how well marked it was, that there were shelters at the end of a day's hike—but she found most of the shelters had been blown down or burned. Much of the time she slept on benches, tables, and on the ground. On bitter cold nights she would heat stones to sleep on.

In places the trail was little more than a path. There were sand and gravel washouts, weeds and brush up to her neck.

But she would not quit. She inched her way over great ledges of shelf rock made slick with sleet, waded across 30-foot-wide mountain streams, whacked with her cane at dense underbrush. She is not afraid of forest animals, although a rattlesnake struck but just got her dungarees.

Mrs. Gatewood is the only woman who ever accomplished this feat. At the top of Mount Katahdin she signed the register and sang "America the Beautiful." In her own words, she was—

Just walking the trail for pleasure
For the love of out of doors,
For the lovely works our Maker
Displays on forest floors.

In an editorial, the *Boston Post* states that Mrs. Emma Gatewood, of Ohio, demonstrated that the hardihood of pioneer women survives today.

The Millinocket, Maine, Chamber of Commerce presented her with a framed picture of Mount Katahdin when she was its guest. She was also awarded a trophy and a life membership in the National Hikers and Campers Association.

Mrs. Gatewood is a relative of O. O. McIntyre, famed New York columnist, whose syndicated columns covering the United States helped make the city of Gallipolis, Ohio, famous.

By the wonderful performance, Mrs. Emma Gatewood has achieved for herself a place with the heroes of the country.

18

AGAIN

On April 12, when she was all alone at home, Emma Gatewood quietly sewed a new bag out of a yard of denim—large enough to carry a few items of clothing, gear, first-aid supplies, and food.

On April 16, she babysat her grandchildren, and they did not behave, and she wrote in her diary, "I will be glad when I can get away."

On April 22, she bought a Timex wristwatch for fourteen dollars and watched a man in the bus station take the screws out of the hinges on a telephone booth with a coin and then walk away.

On April 24, she went to Mrs. Church's house and sat on the porch for a while with Lannie Thompson's little girl, then caught a ride with Ms. JaQuay to Northup, then down the road and past the old family homestead, high on the hill, then on up Raccoon Creek to Edith's place. On the way back, she went to Dr. Allison's to get her false teeth, which were ready for pickup, and to Dr. Thomas's to get a screw for her glasses. Then she packed her suitcase, grabbed her coat, and went up to Monroe's for the night so she could leave bright and early to catch the bus to Charleston, then the plane to Atlanta, then the bus to Jasper, then the taxi to Mount Oglethorpe.

It had been nineteen months since she stood on Mount Katahdin. She'd had two birthday parties and thousands of those little moments that make a civilized, nice, normal life, of rhubarb pie and dirty dishes, of pot roast and burping babies.

Now, two weeks before Mother's Day 1957, six months before her seventieth birthday, the Appalachian Trail was calling her back.

— — — — — —

In May 1957, a journalist named Murray T. Pringle wrote a story for *American Mercury* called "Tried Walking Lately," which pointed out that Americans had become irreversibly dependent on the automobile. "No American generation has walked less than the present one, or has paid less heed to Thomas Jefferson's dictum that 'Of all exercises, walking is the best.'"

— — — — — —

The card arrived at Lucy's house in Columbus, Ohio, postmarked CARATUNK, MAINE.

Sept. 7, 57

Dear Lucy, Louise, et al,

There was a reception of about twenty met me at the river yesterday evening. Two reporters, four forest wardens and others. I think I will be through in ten days. I have taken so much time off to visit or could have been done. I am fine and having the time of my young life. Hoping all is fine with you. I am, with love, Mamma.

— — — — — —

MOUNT KATAHDIN, ME, SEPT. 16 – (AP) – Mrs. Emma Gatewood, a 69-year-old grandmother from Gallipolis, Ohio will climb Mt. Katahdin's 5267-foot peak today after completing her 2026-mile hike along the Appalachian Trail.

It was the second trip along the trail for Mrs. Gatewood. She is the first woman to have completed the journey in its entirety in one season. She started the trip from Mt. Oglethorpe, Ga., April 27, and arrived here yesterday.

— — — — — —

They called her "Queen of the Forest."

In 1955, she was the first woman to thru-hike alone. In 1957, she became the first person—man or woman—to walk the world's longest trail twice. She reached the Katahdin summit nearly blind because her glasses kept fogging over during the climb, so she simply took them off. "I could not see," she wrote in her diary. "It made me plenty nervous getting down over all those rocks, but I slowly made it without accident."

She descended the mountain with a spate of new stories. "Gettin' too old," she told a reporter at the bottom of the mountain. "There were places where I had to pull myself over sheer rocks and I'm afraid I'll get to the age where I won't be able to do that anymore."

She had walked within six feet of a rattlesnake in May, in the Georgia foothills. She backed away, waited ten minutes for the snake to move, then cut around through the woods, leaving the "sassy thing" rattling.

About her lack of nourishment a few days later, she wrote, "I was so tired and my knees felt weak from lack of food, I wobbled when I walked." At her weakest, she approached an unpainted shack to ask for food. Dogs ran out barking and a man with a peg leg appeared on the porch. The place looked so poor that she did not expect to find a meal, but the peg-legged man had heard about Emma's hiking and sent her away with boiled eggs, corn pone, stewed beef, an onion, and a can of condensed milk.

An old mutt followed her from Tennessee to Virginia and into a store, where she bought new shoes and left her old high tops—and the dog.

On June 14, she saw her first bear, coming down the trail. She shouted, "Hey!" and the bear loped off.

She was bitten by something—she didn't know what—near Roanoke and her leg swelled to the knee. It grew so bad that she begged a ride to the doctor. She didn't tell him who she was or what she was doing for fear he'd try to stop her. He gave her penicillin, the first she'd ever had, and also some pink pills he did not identify. She spent the rest of the day on the couch of a stranger who waited on her as though she were an invalid. Her foot ached for days and made walking painful.

On June 27, she walked through Shenandoah National Park in Virginia. "No one recognized me," she wrote in her journal. "Still think I am a tramp."

She spent a solid July day in Pennsylvania not talking to Dorothy Laker, who would become the second woman to thru-hike by herself. "I started before five, but it was not long until [Laker] passed me. I did not talk to her. Then I passed her, on and off, all day, but never saying a word to each other." Laker, in her own account of the day, doesn't mention Emma at all. It's hard to know why the two didn't speak. Competition, maybe?

In August, Emma walked up on a shelter occupied by Boy Scouts and saw their leader sitting outside in his "birthday clothes."

On the best nights, she was greeted warmly by friends she had made two years before and slept on comfortable mattresses in climate-controlled houses. On unlucky nights, she found shelter beside ant-infested logs, or on piles of leaves or grass, or, on one rainy evening, inside a large pasteboard box that surprisingly kept her fairly dry. She slept under the trailer of a long-haul eighteen-wheeler, and in the posh Bear Mountain Inn, and at the Laurel Ridge Tourist Home, where, she wrote, "There was so much noise all night by giggling girls and indecent sounds I did not sleep much. I would liked to have thrown a lot of things down stairs."

She even made her bed one night in the amen corner of an abandoned country church.

In New York, she witnessed an AWOL soldier turn himself in to the state police. In Connecticut, she rode in a parade onboard a fire engine with the volunteer fire department. In several towns where word of her travels arrived early, folks hosted welcoming parties that made Emma feel special. One woman, upon recognizing her, gave Emma a kiss that could be heard around the block.

On the path, the beauty of nature fulfilled her. She gazed at a mountainside violet with a purple tip, like an orchid. She watched a wood-pewee feed her babies in a nest in the corner of a lean-to. A wild turkey crossed her path. She was resting one afternoon on a thick, moss-covered log, daydreaming, when a red fox came jogging down the path, carrying small prey in its mouth, oblivious to the old woman lying on the log. She watched it come near, then asked, "Are you bringing me my dinner?" The fox shot through the forest like a red streak.

She hadn't kept this hike a secret like she had the last. She sent postcards home from Clingmans Dome, in Tennessee.

"She was sending cards to all of us, at different times and from different places," Nelson told me. "She was hiking fourteen miles a day, so we intercepted her. We went up east of Harrisburg, to Lehigh Gap, Pennsylvania, and here she came. We took her to dinner there, and the next morning we hiked up the rock formation called Devil's Pulpit. She was having a good time. She just talked about the trail, told us about things she had run across. Told us about the bear."

She met reporters, too, nearly everywhere she went. Even more so than the first trip, this journey was well-documented in American newspapers, magazines, and on television.

"Some people think it's crazy," she told one reporter. "But I find a restfulness—something that satisfies my type of nature. The woods make me feel more contented."

"What made you do all this?" a reporter asked.

"The forest is a quiet place and nature is beautiful. I don't want to sit and rock. I want to do something."

She told them she found the trail in better condition that year. Her initial criticism had prompted hiking clubs to clean and mark parts of the trail. That was also part of the reason she finished the hike in fewer days.

Before she left Millinocket, the chamber of commerce presented her with a blue and gray suit. She spoke to the students and teachers at the local high school. She spent part of one day baking special cookies, then delivered them to patients at the Millinocket Community Hospital.

Back home in Gallia County, she was the talk of the town. The Blue Devil marching band played theme music to honor her at a Friday night football game. The chamber of commerce presented her a plaque at halftime and declared it "Grandma Gatewood Night."

"I'd like to go to the South Pole," she told a group of Gallipolis Rotarians who invited her to speak, "but nobody'll take me there. There's no need for old ladies at the South Pole. I guess they have their own cooks."

The Queen of the Forest posed with politicians and told her story at school assemblies. She addressed the Palmerton Over 60 Club and the League of Ohio Sportsmen and welcomed even more reporters to sit and chat.

"Mrs. Gatewood possesses a wonderful sense of humor," one wrote. "She reports having had a good laugh all by herself near the beginning of her hike. She had lain down to rest under a tree and after a bit, quite unconsciously moved her arm and frightened away a buzzard that was about to light. She thought to herself, 'I'm not ready to have my bones picked yet.'"

With the second A.T. hike complete, she began striking out elsewhere. She spent eight days and nights on the Baker Trail in

Pennsylvania, and when she stopped in Aspinwall on the Allegheny River, she spent three weeks at the Redwing Girl Scout camp, chopping trees, setting up tents, and preparing the camp for winter. She was invited to a weeklong retreat at Canter's Cave 4-H camp in Ohio, forty-three miles from her home. She walked there.

In 1958, at age seventy, she climbed six mountains in the Adirondack Range and expressed interest in joining the Forty-Sixers, a club of men who had climbed all forty-six Adirondack peaks of more than four thousand feet. Occasionally she'd ask a young relative or friend to accompany her, but she was careful not to bend societal norms. When an older man asked to join her on an extended hike, she declined. *People would talk*, she said. She had become an evangelist for walking, for experiencing nature, at a time when pedestrianism in America was in steep decline. She wrote of its benefits often in flowery poems.

"The Reward of Nature"

If you'll go with me to the mountains
And sleep on the leaf carpeted floors
And enjoy the bigness of nature
And the beauty of all out-of-doors,
You'll find your troubles all fading
And feel the Creator was not man
That made lovely mountains and forests
Which only a Supreme Power can.

When we trust in the Power above
And with the realm of nature hold fast,
We will have a jewel of great price
To brighten our lives till the last.

For the love of nature is healing,
If we will only give it a try
And our reward will be forthcoming,
If we go deeper than what meets the eye.

She didn't reveal her plans for the next big hike, but soon enough everyone would know.

Sitting beside Sunfish Lake, New Jersey, near the Delaware Water Gap, age sixty-nine, 1958. Courtesy Lucy Gatewood Seeds

19

PIONEER WOMAN

1959

The streets of Portland were packed. Traffic was backed up in all directions. There was a maelstrom of cars, horses, dogs, bicycles, and people, some five thousand of them, many with white hair, waiting in the August heat on the little old woman to walk down Sandy Boulevard, through the gold ribbon stretched across the intersection of Eighty-Second Avenue.

A cheer went up when Emma Gatewood came into view. She was flanked by several hundred elderly citizens, some of them clad in pioneer-era clothing, who had hiked the last few miles with her.

The seventy-one-year-old woman looked tired. Spent. Her skin was leathery and tanned to a deep bronze. The soles of her shoes were worn thin. She seemed ready to collapse.

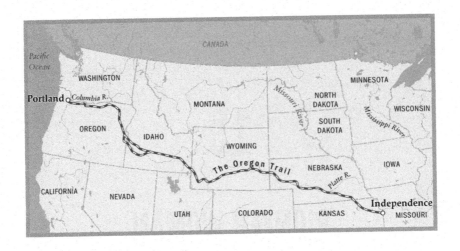

The press had been speculating for days that she wouldn't make it to her goal. A rumor spread that she had accepted a ride, and this became a sign that she might abandon her walk short of her destination.

GRANDMA'S TRAIL-WEARY, proclaimed the *Miami News*.

RIDE, REST HINT WALK MIGHT END, read the headline in the *Spokane Daily Chronicle*.

WALKING GRANDMA MAY GIVE UP GOAL, shouted the *Toledo Blade*.

Indeed, it had been a grueling trip. This wasn't the Appalachian Trail, with its shade trees and beautiful vistas and cold-water springs. Those were scarce between Independence, Missouri, and Portland, Oregon. In ninety-five days she had walked at three miles per hour on scalding asphalt through Missouri, Kansas, Nebraska, Wyoming, Idaho, and Oregon carrying a blue umbrella she bought for $1.50 to protect her from the sun. It had survived the entire trip in spite of the passing trucks that tried to rip it from her hands, and it came to be a symbol for guts and determination.

She did her best to stick to the Old Oregon Trail, which was blazed by trappers and traders and pioneers in the early 1800s and served as the main route for a half million settlers seeking a better life in the West. In Vale, Oregon, she even took time to visit the grave of John D. Henderson, an immigrant who died of thirst, or maybe the black measles, in 1852, in the desert between the Malheur River and Snake River. The story has it that his team died not long into the trip from Independence. Henderson decided to continue on foot, but he couldn't make it. A blacksmith chiseled his name into stone and pressed on.

The idea to walk the trail had come to her while reading about the Oregon Centennial Exposition. She had spent a chunk of 1958 hiking other pieces of the Appalachian Trail, intending to string together a third two-thousand-mile hike in sections. She had walked from Duncannon, Pennsylvania, to North Adams, Massachusetts. A hike west was indeed a change of scenery.

"I read a piece in the newspapers about that wagon train going to Oregon [in conjunction with the exposition], and I thought of all the women who walked behind the wagons when they went to settle the country," she told a reporter in Junction City, Kansas. "I was looking for something to do this summer and a walk to Oregon seemed like the best thing."

She left Independence, Missouri, on May 4, two weeks after former president Harry Truman waved good-bye to the seven-wagon train, and plodded through the plains. She sent a postcard home from Denver, Colorado, on June 3, saying that the snow on the mountains was beautiful and that the governor of Oregon had made her a goodwill ambassador at large and that she was staying with some folks who stopped her on the road. "I am fine," she wrote. She passed the wagon train a month later, in Pocatello, Idaho, but the journey had been difficult. She slept outdoors in the Wyoming sagebrush on fourteen nights.

The newspapers called her "America's most celebrated pedestrian" and printed updates along the way, and again people across the country started pulling for the grandma who wouldn't stop walking.

"My legs go mechanical-like," she told one reporter. "When someone stops me, I have to make an effort to get them going again."

Emma mailed a letter to Lucy in Columbus on July 27, when she arrived in Meacham, Oregon. "Things are getting quite exciting for me," she wrote.

> I went to a rodeo . . . where there was ten thousand fans and was introduced over the loudspeaker and stood up and waved with the floodlights on me. When I came to a two-lane bridge several hundred feet long across the Snake River, the Highway Patrol held up the traffic one way while I walked across. I felt like Royalty. The Patrol are keeping close watch to see that I do not come to harm. A man from the Centennial Staff met me on the highway and gave me a pass and said I would have a car with chauffeur to use, get all the clothes I needed, have a hotel with all expenses paid, and one day of the Centennial would be proclaimed Emma or Grandma Gatewood day. From what I hear from there, there will be other favors. I am a little excited but not losing any sleep over it. I wish you could be here to enjoy it with me. I have 250 miles to go yet. Folks are doing everything for me. They came to help me have a pleasant trip. Things are very pretty here. After all the treeless country, they surely look good. I will get to Pendleton tomorrow and will soon be going down the Columbia River, which I am told is very beautiful. I was given a dress, shoes, and suitcase at Baker and they have been sent by the Chamber of Commerce on to Portland. I will be getting mail in Portland addressed General Delivery if you want to write. Hoping all is fine there. I am, with love, Mamma.

Large groups in Oregon anticipating her arrival began to gather roadside and cheer her through. Even the trainman on a passing caboose waved and asked her if she wanted a ride.

Her patience was tested when she began to be badgered by people who wanted to take her picture and ask her the same set of questions. The attention had begun to grate, and by the end her emotions were ragged. She told one reporter that she felt like a "sideshow freak." She began to approach crowds with her head bowed and a handkerchief covering part of her face.

West of Meacham, near La Grande, a bevy of motorists stopped her beside the road, but as they snapped pictures and rattled off a flurry of questions, she simply walked away. Farther west, outside The Dalles, she threw stones at a pesky newsman. Near Hood River, a few days before she got to Portland, a young photographer approached her and squatted to take her picture. She swung her umbrella and struck him on the forehead, leaving a big red welt and drawing blood. In the articles that ran the next day, Emma was called "peppery" and the photographer was quoted saying she "hit like a mule."

"She let me have it," the photographer, Robert Hall, told reporters. "But when she saw the blood on my face, she cried and said she felt awful. I told her all was forgotten."

Someone brought her a lawn chair, a hamburger, and a glass of ice water, and she calmed down. She even hugged Robert Hall. All was forgiven.

Now, on August 7, nearly two thousand miles from where she started, she walked the last short stretch into Portland at a clip that had the Centennial greeters, news reporters, and other well-wishers gasping for breath. The city was buzzing. Portland politicians had declared it Grandma Gatewood Day and boosters had greeted her with flowers at the city line. Police had blocked off a lane of traffic to allow Emma, and the hundreds now walking with her, safe passage. The traffic jam, according to a reporter for the *Oregonian*, was unprecedented.

When Emma reached the ribbon, she was overcome with tears. She brushed it apart and fell into the arms of a stranger and wept. She seemed shaken by it all, particularly the crowds. She climbed into a police car with Capt. John Pittenger to get away from the crush for a few minutes. When she had regained her composure, she returned to the intersection and got into the back of a red Oldsmobile convertible and, beaming, rode off in a motorcade toward the exposition grounds.

"Who do they think I am?" she asked the mayor of Portland. "Queen Elizabeth?"

She showered and traded in her faded and torn cotton blouse and skirt for a donated dress, an Evelyn Gibson French blue crepe with a pale pink Alençon lace yoke and matching jacket. She donned a blue hat and white gloves and carried a new purse. The outfit was provided for free, as was a lunch of salad, crab cocktail, and well-done roast beef, which she ate with the mayor and police chief. Emma took one shoe off while they ate, but nobody seemed to mind. Her old clothes and the umbrella were taken for an exhibit at the museum of history.

Presents poured in from all corners. She was given the key to Portland. Someone donated a new umbrella. Someone else a watch. She accepted a corsage and gold plaque from the East Broadway Boosters. She got a big basket of fruit from the Hollywood Boosters, then took a ride over the city in a bright yellow helicopter. As she climbed off the helicopter, a woman approached to take her picture and Emma knocked the camera to the ground and immediately felt bad. She apologized dramatically, saying she was still vexed by the great hordes of people who wanted her picture.

The city of Portland put her up at the luxurious Hotel Benson, where she was pampered. Overwhelmed as she was, she seemed pleased by all the attention. She was invited to Hollywood and hammed it up on Art Linkletter's *House Party*. She was alternatively the guest of the Oregon Centennial Commission, the Oregon Coast Association, and others who showed her around the state. They drove her to the coast where a group of colorfully dressed Coos Bay Pirates surprised her and presented her with a scarf. She was whisked to Medford, waded in the Pacific at Seaside, piloted a fifty-two-foot Coast Guard rescue boat near Newport, fished for salmon at Gold Beach, and rode the mail boat to Agness. Nearly everywhere she went she got a key to the city. A month later, when it was time to leave, the bus company gave her an open ticket, fixed so she could stop anywhere along the line through Seattle, Spokane, Glacier National Park, Winnipeg, Chicago, Detroit, Columbus, and Gallipolis.

She was everyone's grandma now.

At the end of the year, when the United Press in Oregon put together its list of the biggest news of 1959, it included stories about the Portland newspaper strike, the collision of two jets over Mount Hood, the successful separation of Siamese twins, the discovery of two bodies in the Columbia River, and the kidnapping of the Harrisburg police chief. At number two on the list, just below a story about the combustion of a truck laden with six tons of explosives in downtown Roseburg that killed thirteen citizens and caused ten million dollars in damage, was the Oregon Centennial and the following line: "An Ohio grandmother, Mrs. Emma Gatewood, hiked on foot all the way to Portland."

— — — — —

In November 1959, two months after she'd headed for home, Emma was invited back to the NBC Studios in Hollywood to be a special guest on Groucho Marx's television quiz show *You Bet Your Life* alongside author Max Shulman, who wrote the Dobie Gillis stories and had just released a Dobie Gillis novel called *I Was a Teen-Age Dwarf*. In an episode that aired the following January, Emma appeared from behind a wall and walked sheepishly across the stage as the audience politely clapped. She wore a pearl choker, dark medium-heeled shoes, a plain dress, and a short jacket. Her thick glasses magnified her eyes. She reached out and shook Marx's hand.

"Emma, I'm delighted to meet you," he said. "And Max, of course I've known you for some time. Now, where are you from, Emma?"

"Gallipolis, Ohio," she says.

"Gallipolis, Ohio?"

"Yes."

"Isn't there a famous writer who came from there?"

"McIntyre," she said.

"O. O. McIntyre, yeah," Groucho said. "See what a memory I have for trivia?"

"Mm-hmm."

"He was a very good columnist in his day. He always talked about Gallipolis, but I notice he lived in New York," Groucho said as the audience giggled. "He was always talking about Gallipolis. Were you born on a farm, Emma?"

"Yes, I was."

"Why was this?" he said. "I mean, what did your folks raise on the farm in addition to you?"

"Tobacco, corn, wheat, and a little Cain," she said, smiling slyly.

"A little Cain?" Groucho said.

Emma giggled.

"How big a family did he raise, Emma?"

"Fifteen."

"Fifteen? Well he must've raised quite some Cain."

She laughed with her lips sealed, like she was trying to hide her teeth.

"You think fifteen children in one family is a good idea?" Groucho said. "Would you recommend it—"

"No."

"—to other parents?"

"No," she said. "That's too many. They can't take proper care of 'em."

"Do you have children?"

"I have eleven," Emma said.

"In other words, you don't subscribe to your own philosophy, do you?" Groucho asked, looking sideways at the audience.

Groucho turned to Shulman.

"There's one thing in your book that I find extremely interesting, Max. You say that our society has developed a matriarchy. Would you explain this in detail for Emma here?"

"Oh, certainly," Shulman said. "I'd be happy to. This is a country run by women, without question."

"You'll get no argument out of me," Groucho said.

"When you and I were boys, when Dad came home at night, no matter how hard he'd been working during the day, he could depend on it that Mama was more tired than he, because she had been baking bread and scrubbing clothes by hand and making soap and cooking dinner. But today, with automatic washers and driers and store bread and TV dinners and power steering, he comes home at night, he's just dragging himself into the house and she looks as though she's spent a month in the country. She's full of plans. She says, 'Dear, don't you think we ought to flood the study and make an aquarium out of it?' Or, 'Don't you think we ought to put another set of braces on Peter's teeth?' You know, things like that. Now this poor tired man lying there says, 'You decide, honey.' Well, you give a woman power like that and she's bound to achieve the size to go with it."

"There's no doubt about this," Groucho said. "The women are in the driver's seat."

"But I must say, I don't think women like it that way," said Shulman.

"I don't think so either. I think they're very insecure," Groucho said.

"They would prefer the men to run the home and the country," Shulman said.

"But the men have relinquished."

"That's right."

"They have capitulated."

"The women have gotten it by default."

"That's right."

"So nobody's happy," Shulman said. "The men don't want it. The women don't want it. And the kids don't know who their fathers are."

At this the audience laughed.

"Now, Emma, what about you?" Groucho said. "You've been listening to this sophomoric conversation here. Do you think it's a good idea for the wife to run the family?"

Emma closed her eyes and paused for a second or two.

"Nope."

"Well, Emma, now that your children are grown, what do you do for excitement?"

"Oh, I hike," she said.

"You *hike?*"

"Yes."

"You mean you just keep walking. What kind of walking do you do?"

"I walked the Oregon Trail."

"The *Oregon Trail?* You walked it?" he said.

"Yes, I walked it."

"You mean like Lewis and Clark?"

"Yes."

"When was this?"

"This year."

"You walked the Oregon Trail this year," Groucho said. "How did you arrive at that kind of a pastime?"

"Oh, I didn't have anything else to do," she said. "The family is all married and gone and I just wanted to do something."

"How old are you?"

"Seventy-two."

"Seventy-two? And how long was this trip that you . . ."

"Two thousand miles."

Gasps spread across the room. One person in the audience began clapping. More joined in and the applause rose. Emma's expression was blank. She looked at the ground and swayed just a little.

"What were you walking for?" Groucho asked.

"Well, I like to walk . . ."

"When you got to the other end, what happened? Did you turn around and walk back again?"

"No. This year I walked up to the Centennial, up to Portland."

"From where?"

"Independence, Missouri."

"Oh, my," said a woman in the audience. A man whistled and another began to clap. A low chatter commenced and you could picture the audience turning to each other mid-gasp, awed by this woman who now had a small smile on her lips.

— — — — —

Back home in Gallia County, Emma collected a few paw-paw seeds and buckeyes and put them in a pouch with a card addressed for Portland Mayor Terry Schrunk. She wrote that she enjoyed her visit. Alas, like many settlers before, she wrote, "My family are all here and I supposed I will remain here."

Well. Sort of. Home was more like home base.

20

BLAZING

1960–1968

"She's sitting right over there." The bus terminal manager pointed across the room, toward the thick Thursday afternoon crowd. "The lady in the blue coat."

The reporter walked through the bus station, toward the seventy-two-year-old woman wearing white gloves, a white blouse, thick glasses, and a winter hat to keep her ears warm against the February cold. She seemed impatient. She'd been sitting a while. The reporter introduced himself.

"If that bus doesn't come soon," she said, "I'm going to walk to Dayton."

Emma was in Chillicothe, Ohio, trying to catch a ride. She had to be in Cincinnati by Saturday and wanted to visit her son, Nelson, before then.

The reporter asked the standard questions, the ones she'd answered a thousand times. *Why do you hike? Why do you hike alone? How do you survive in the wild?* She told him she'd been named a lifetime member of the National Campers and Hikers Association and that she was working on establishing hiking trails through the Ohio hills. A few months before, the executive committee of a nonprofit called Buckeye Trail, Inc., of which she was a charter member, had received permission from the state to begin marking a trail from Lake Erie south through the Zaleski State Forest and on to Cincinnati. The blazing was expected to take four or five years. "The nation's most famous trail walker," the *Columbus Dispatch* had called her in a story about the effort.

The reporter asked how she kept in good enough shape to blaze trails.

"Exercise is most important," she said. "Too many people hop in the car to go two blocks for a bar of soap."

Where was she headed now? he asked.

"I've always wanted to ride on a boat," she said.

A letter came to Lucy on February 24, 1960. Emma was aboard the *Delta Queen*, a Mississippi River steamboat, heading from Cincinnati to New Orleans for Mardi Gras with 130 passengers from fifteen states and Canada. The night before, docked in Memphis, the *Delta Queen* calliope premiered. Five thousand people and the mayor of Memphis stood on the banks to listen. "It has been a nice trip so far," she wrote. "We have a masquerade party tonight."

Two months later, on April 28, she set out from Springer Mountain in Georgia, the new southern terminus of the Appalachian Trail, to try to complete her third A.T. hike. She had to abandon the hike after seventy-five miles, at Deep Gap, North Carolina, because of a massive blowdown. "It would take 100 men three months to cut their way through that," she told the local paper.

On June 2, she was photographed hiking along the eighty-five-mile Horseshoe Trail near Hershey, Pennsylvania, where she had asked a group of boys if they had any food.

Thirteen days later, on June 15, a reporter found her ninety-five miles away, in Wind Gap, Pennsylvania. She told him she was headed "vaguely north," maybe to Canada.

"You look strong," the reporter told her.

"What did you expect?" Emma replied.

He asked if she kept her children in the loop with postcards.

"I write to 'em," she said, "but I don't tell 'em nothing. I don't see any use in making a big fuss about it. I just do what I want to do."

A week later, she was at her daughter Lucy's door, in White Plains, New York, telling of the porcupine that tried to sleep on her feet and the rat she kicked away while she slept against a stone wall.

Two weeks later, a resident of Cheshire, Massachusetts, phoned the local newspaper to report that the "tough as a nail" hiking grandmother had just left her home for the summit of nearby Mount Greylock, the highest point in the state, the peak coveted by Nathaniel Hawthorne, Herman Melville, and Henry David Thoreau.

A few days later, the *North Adams Transcript* reported that "the great-grandmother of the hiking fraternity" paid for a fifteen-minute airplane ride so she could see the Appalachian Trail from above.

Twenty-three days later, on August 7—one year to the day from when she finished the Oregon Trail—Emma crossed the border into Canada, the Long Trail of Vermont behind her. There were no cheering crowds. Just trees. She was happy nonetheless. She scratched out a letter and sent it to the folks back home.

> It was a hard trip, but in spite of all the obstacles I stuck it out to the end. Some of those mountains are quite a challenge for one my age, and I wondered a lot of times whether I could

make it, but I kept putting one foot ahead of the other until I got to Canada. I did not sleep out as there are plenty of cabins and shelters. Only three times was there anyone in camp with me. There were two boys who started from the north but will not go far I imagine, as they were too lazy to get up and start in the morning. One has to work hard at it if they are to get far. I hiked alone the entire trip, but I took my time so that I did not hurt myself in any way. I saw a bear and a cub on Breadloaf Mountain. The cub went up a tree and the mother pranced around going "whup, whup." I was about 30 feet from them and they were too near the trail for me to pass. I went back and sat on a rock for a few minutes and they went away. I roasted a porcupine that I killed. I first threw him in the fire and got all the quills off, then I skinned the thing. It looked all right and did not smell bad. It had such a nice liver so I put it on a stick and roasted it, salted it and cut off a bite, took one or two chews on it and spit it out. It took me two or three days to get that taste out of my mouth. I had the porky over the fire, and after the liver my imagination got the better of me and I dropped the thing in the fire and burned him up.

Altogether I have hiked about 700 miles this year and wore out two pairs of tennis shoes. I cannot see that the trip hurt me any. I am now seventy-two years old and able to do a lot more hiking.

— — — — —

In 1960, as Emma Gatewood covered the country by boat and plane and mostly on her own two feet, something strange was happening. That April, two British paratroopers—Sgt. Patrick Maloney, thirty-four, and Sgt. Mervyn Evans, thirty-three—left San Francisco on a walk to New York. They aimed to make the trip in seventy days in an attempt to break the cross-country record of seventy-nine days, which had stood since 1926.

This was not long after J. M. Flagler, writing for the *New Yorker*, bemoaned the loss of long-walker Edward Weston and American pedestrians of his day. "Nowadays," he wrote, "distance, endurance, and speed walking are all but lost arts in America."

The pedestrian headlines were back, and the paratroopers weren't the only ones making them. Walking behind the two soldiers was Dr. Barbara Moore, a British vegetarian who embarked on the 3,250-mile walk to show that her diet of fruits, vegetables, and grass juice were better for endurance than an American diet of meat and coffee. The doctor claimed that she had cured herself of leukemia with an experimental diet. She said she planned to have a baby at age 100, and live to be 150.

Somewhere along the route, the vegetarian, who was accompanied most of the way by a supply-laden car, vowed to beat the paratroopers to New York. She passed them at least once out West, as they slept, but the men, who swore they weren't racing, soon pulled ahead. They gained a larger lead when Moore was struck by a car and hospitalized in Brazil, Indiana.

By the time the paratroopers made it to Bethlehem, Pennsylvania, the vegetarian was lobbing accusations that they had cheated by hitching rides. She told reporters she had affidavits stating they had caught rides for nearly a third of the way. The two men finished in sixty-six days, shattering the record. Moore limped into Times Square and into throngs of onlookers after a rough eighty-five days of walking, complaining that the paratroopers had taken an easier route.

Emma knew about the paratroopers and told a reporter that she'd like to meet them. What about Moore? "Some people think I ought to make it a point to see her," Emma said, "but I don't think we'd agree on anything."

Something new was afoot, though. *Newsweek* sniffed it out the same year. A fad was sweeping the United Kingdom: distance walking. It wasn't just the vegetarian and the paratroopers. One man had walked 110 miles from Norwich to London in thirty hours. After that, 250 women representing armed forces auxiliaries walked from Birmingham to London. A chronometer factory owner in Saint Albans who thought kids were sissies challenged his four hundred male employees to walk fifty miles in fifteen hours. Thirty-two tried, and sixteen finished.

The United States was a little slow to catch on, but by 1963, distance walking was taking the country by storm. "The Marines are marching. Girls are marching. Practically everyone is marching," wrote the Associated Press in February. The hoopla began when Marine Commandant Gen. David M. Shoup unearthed a long-forgotten executive order from President Theodore Roosevelt that prescribed fitness standards for marines. In 1908, Roosevelt felt the marines should be in good enough shape to walk fifty miles in three days, with a total of twenty hours' rest. Shoup sent the document to President John F. Kennedy as a historic courtesy. Kennedy wondered whether modern marines could pass the test, and in a matter of hours, marine headquarters issued a directive ordering a test by officers of the 2nd Marine Division at Camp Lejeune, North Carolina. Kennedy casually noted in a letter to Shoup that Roosevelt "laid down such requirements not only for the officers of the Marine Corps but, when possible, for members of his own family, members of his staff and cabinet, and even for unlucky foreign diplomats who were dragooned into hiking with him through Washington's Rock Creek Park." Furthermore, he wrote, if the test indicates "that the strength and stamina of the modern Marine is at least equivalent to that of his antecedents, I will then ask Mr. Salinger to look into the matter personally and give me a report on the fitness of the White House staff."

As soon as word of the challenge got out, people across the country, strangely, started walking, aiming at fifty miles. Boy Scouts hiked in Illinois. Secretaries sauntered in Washington, DC. Students at Stanford University set out. Politicians looking for headlines took off with reporters trailing them. Four hundred high school kids in Marion County, California, tried for fifty miles and ninety-seven of them finished, including nineteen girls. Attorney General Robert Kennedy finished fifty miles in seventeen hours and fifty minutes.

"Heel blisters became the hash-marks of the New Frontier," reported the United Press.

"Walking, an almost forgotten art in this motor-made nation, suddenly became as important as goldfish swallowing once was," read an Associated Press dispatch.

"The big surprise was the reaction in the infinitely mysterious chemistry of the American people," said a story in *Newsweek*. "Citizens of all ages and conditions, mostly flabby, went after the 50-mile mark in one of the woolliest of pursuits since men first chased wild geese."

— — — — — —

In May 1963, a man named Paris Whitehead was walking along the trail in Shenandoah National Park when he looked up and saw an elderly woman walking toward him. She wore a hat, tennis shoes, and a plastic raincoat. She was carrying a bundle. She was so wild looking that he knew exactly who she was. Queen of the Appalachian Trail, Grandma Gatewood. He had heard all about her. He knew she had walked the trail twice and had slept in more homes than George Washington. He'd later tell a friend about the experience, and Ronald Strickland would write of the encounter in his book, *Pathfinder*: "Knowing of her experience through all sections of the Trail, I asked her which part she liked best. 'Going downhill, Sonny,' she replied."

— — — — — —

Late in the summer of 1964, Merrill C. Gilfillan, an Ohio con-
servationist who was doing a feature story for *Columbus Dispatch
Magazine* showed up at the Pinkham Notch Hut south of Gorham, New Hampshire. He had arranged to meet up there with
Emma Gatewood, who was trying to finish hiking the Appalachian
Trail for the third time. When she didn't show the first day, he .
was mildly concerned. His worry grew on the second day as temperatures in the valleys of the Presidential Range dropped below
thirty degrees. The third day brought snow above the timberline
and winds of fifty to sixty miles per hour. By the fourth day, he
was truly alarmed. He spoke to the director of the Appalachian
Mountain Club hut system, who began a radio check of the huts
in an effort to find Grandma. He tried several times but couldn't
track her down. The director felt it was time to ask for a search. He
was just about to call the US Forest Service when he found her, at
Mizpah Spring Shelter, a few miles above Crawford Notch. They'd
meet soon.

While Gilfillan waited on her to arrive, he watched as hundreds
of hikers came and went. The hut master said some two hundred
a day passed through. Most were college age, wearing the newest
clothes and carrying the best backpacks and gear.

The contrast was remarkable as Emma appeared out of the
spruce and walked through the rain, wearing a sheepskin vest and
serviceable gloves she'd found on the trail, and carrying her sack
over her shoulder. She was recognized by the younger hikers coming
through. They flocked around her, asking questions about the trail,
showing honest admiration.

She was damaged, though. She had fallen her first day out and
hurt her knee. The injury slowed her so much she couldn't make it
to shelter and slept outdoors that night. A few days later, she was

attacked by a German shepherd, which bit her on the leg before she could drive it away with her stick. She still had a nasty wound.

What struck Gilfillan was that she was happy. The bumps and bites didn't seem to bother her. She wore a smile and a subtle look of determination.

"After the hard life I have lived," she said, "this trail isn't so bad."

— — — — — —

On September 17, 1964, having traversed again one of the most difficult A.T. stretches, through Vermont, New Hampshire, and Maine; having survived the final day of walking on bullion cubes and a handful of peanuts; Emma Gatewood, seventy-seven, reached Rainbow Lake, a fitting place to complete her third hike, since she had walked there from Mount Katahdin ten years before, in 1954.

She was the first person to walk the entire trail three times.

The newspapers called her "the female hiking champion of the United States—maybe of the world" and "the famed hiker from Ohio" and "the nation's most famous woman hiker" and "a living legend among hikers." As was customary, she offered criticism, saying that the trail was bad in a few spots—but fewer than the last time she'd been through.

Asked why she liked to hike, she told reporters, "I took it up as kind of a lark."

— — — — —

She sold her house and used the money to buy a small trailer court back in the Gallia County town of Cheshire. The upkeep on the place was hard. Tenants left trash and rags and bottles outside, so she'd clean up and trim around the skirts with a butcher knife while they were away. When her gas mower broke down, she cut the grass with a push mower. She quilted and braided rugs and wrote letters and spoke at school assemblies and washed the windows at the Methodist church.

She captured in her diary the extraordinary minutiae of her twilight.

May 19, 1967.

I took a mattock and shovel and worked on the road around the court; dug a ditch to let the water out, and dug the high places into the holes. Lifted the grass around where the well was dug and wheeled five loads of dirt and filled in. Then put the sod back and watered it and beat it down with the shovel. Put the block of walk back in place. Spaded and planted two hills of cukes, two of pumpkins, four hills of peanuts. Put a fence around to keep the rabbits out. Burned the trash. Got some asparagus down the track and picked lettuce and a few strawberries. Went to the P.O. Fixed the underpinning. And I'm tired.

She continued to travel, especially to annual conventions of the National Campers and Hikers Association, which sometimes drew ten thousand outdoorsmen, and she was routinely singled out by the press.

"People just can't believe an old woman is hiking," she told a reporter at the *Salina Journal* at a meeting in Kansas. "No one would do a thing like that, they figure, unless she was getting paid for it. It's a funny thing. I work like a horse around the trailer court. But when I say I'm taking a hike, they say I shouldn't because I'm too old. I got up on the roof awhile back and sawed off a tree limb. But no one said anything about that."

Back home, she began marking and blazing a hiking trail through Gallia County with the idea it would one day be connected to

*At a meeting of the National Campers
and Hikers Association, 1965.* Courtesy Lucy Gatewood Seeds

the Buckeye Trail, proposed to run between Cincinnati and Lake Erie. She scouted and cleared some thirty miles along the Ohio River, painting trees with robin's egg–blue blazes, two inches wide by six inches long. She negotiated with farmers for permission to cross their private property and built stiles out of logs and rock for climbing barbed-wire fences. At eighty-two, she could be found working on the trail from 7:00 AM to 6:00 PM, alone in the woods. "They said I was too old when I tried to get a job," she told a local reporter. "Why, I've done more since I was 'too old' than most young women."

Cincinnati, 1971. Courtesy Lucy Gatewood Seeds

For her work, Ohio Gov. James Rhodes gave her the State Conservation Award at the Ohio Achievement Day celebration at the
fairgrounds in Columbus. She then flew to Fontana Dam, North
Carolina, where she was a special guest at Fall Colors Hiking Week.

Even with all the attention and honors, she continued to find
peace in nature all by herself. She would stalk the countryside in
search of rare flowers or a dogwood in full bloom. "I went to the
hills today, looking for wild crabapples," she wrote to her daughter.

"I found trailing arbutus all over the place, and a deep wooded gorge I would like to explore."

P. C. Gatewood fell ill in 1968. In his old age, he had been a doting grandfather, and had served as mayor of the tiny village of Crown City for several terms. He is remembered by many as a fair and hardworking man, and a loving grandfather and great-grandfather. His own children had limited contact with him. Several of them confronted him individually about what he had done to their mother, about what they had seen and heard. He claimed to

Near Fontana Dam, 1970. Courtesy Lucy Gatewood Seeds

have no memory of it. No one recalls whether P.C. ever mentioned Emma's notoriety, but they agree he must have known.

According to his son Nelson, he made one dying request in his final days. He wanted to see Emma. He wanted her to come stand in his doorway, just for a moment.

The woman who had walked more than ten thousand miles since she left him refused to take those steps.

— — — — — —

Her family did not attempt to keep tabs on her whereabouts. She'd simply disappear from Gallia County and return home with a new batch of stories.

"Saw an Indian on one of my hikes," she told a reporter in Huntington, chuckling, in 1972.

Last summer, up back of Rutland. I had climbed the ridge and started down the other side. Just as I placed a limb across the fence, I looked up and saw a man in the woods. He had a gun. I hadn't lived this long only to end up being shot in the woods, so I said, "Don't shoot. I'm Grandma Gatewood. I tromp these woods all the time." I could tell by his features that he was an Indian, at least part, and his expression showed that he had never heard of anyone by the name of Gatewood. Pretty soon another fellow came up. He told me they came from Portsmouth, were hunting grouse, and sure enough, the man with him was part Indian. "He knows more about the woods than anyone I know," he said. The first man smiled, looked at me and said, "I've seen lots of things in the woods but you're the most unusual sight I've ever come across."

She added distance to her total tally until she had walked more than fourteen thousand miles, more than halfway around the earth, putting her in the slim company of astonishing pedestrians.

21

MONUMENTS

1973

If there was one place Emma loved, it was a deep and breathtaking sandstone gorge in the hills of southeastern Ohio, a place called Old Man's Cave, which was carved by streams and percolating ground-water. Through the gorge, the stream snakes through a gallery of features, including waterfalls and eddy pools, diving one hundred feet in half a mile. The moist and cool hollow preserves typically northern trees such as the eastern hemlock and Canada yew, which have survived since the glaciers retreated thousands of years ago.

In the winter, the falls freeze over, creating beautiful ice formations.

The gorge is called Old Man's Cave because it was once home to a recluse named Richard Rowe. Rowe had worked for his father's trading business on the Ohio River until the early 1800s, when he

took to the woods to live in solitude. There came a time when he disappeared for several years and was presumed dead. But then he returned. He told an acquaintance he had walked to the Ozark Mountains to find his older brother, but learned he was dead. Rowe told his brother's widow that he had buried a stash of gold in a gorge in Hocking Hills, and that he would fetch it and return to take care of her. Back at his cave, he went out one morning to get a drink of water. He used the butt of his musket to break the ice and it discharged under his chin. Trappers found his body a few days later, wrapped him in bark and buried him on a sandy ledge at Old Man's Cave.

"They're beautiful, those cliffs," Emma once said. "In fact, I think it's more interesting than anything I saw on the Appalachian Trail."

Every January, starting in 1967, she put on her red beret and led a six-mile hike through Hocking Hills, down by Old Man's Cave. People came from across the state. She made lots of new friends. In 1972, when she was eighty-four, it was her job again to lead, to set the pace, but she was having trouble coming down. Her legs bothered her below the knees, mostly down the back. She had been trying to work the pain away with exercise, but she couldn't overcome it. "I feel like taking off to the woods," she'd tell a woman a few months later, "but I don't know whether I'd get back." The trail by Old Man's Cave is steep in spots, and one must climb gnarled tree roots that grow alongside the path. Age was finally wearing her down. She tried to traverse the winter landscape and struggled.

When she could no longer do it safely, several men carried her over the rough spots.

— — — — — —

The following year, 1973, sensing it might be her last event, the organizers held the winter hike in her honor. They made her a hostess, and she stood at the trailhead in her signature beret, greeting her old friends. More than twenty-five hundred hikers showed up. At the lunch break, she was presented the Governor's Community Action Award for her "outstanding contributions to outdoor recreation in Ohio."

She took a bus trip that spring, with an open-ended eighty-five-dollar ticket, visiting forty-eight states and three Canadian provinces. She met friends or family nearly everywhere she went.

She sent a postcard home in May. Pictured on the front was the Pennsylvania Turnpike, "the World's Most Scenic Highway." Her handwriting was shaky. "Am having a nice trip," she wrote. She stopped in Falls Church, Virginia, to visit Ed Garvey, who penned a popular book, *Appalachian Hiker: Adventure of a Lifetime*, about his thru-hike in 1970. She told him about the night on top of a moss-covered mountain she couldn't remember the name of, when the stars looked like a million pinpricks of light in a blanket of darkness.

"It was just as clear, and it looked like I could almost reach out and get the stars, and pull them down," she said. "Oh, I lay there and watched them. It looked so, it was so nice, and it was. . . . Oh, I enjoyed that night. The little old growth on there was just about so high and just as thick as it could be. There's a lot of little pines around there, and I got down, I got down to sort of break the wind, you know? I'll tell you, that was a nice night. I lay there and looked at those stars, and that moon."

On the last leg of the bus trip, in Florida, she felt air conditioning for the first time, and it was cold and unnatural upon her skin. She felt slightly ill when she got home in late May and blamed it on the artificial cool of the bus. It did not slow her. She prepared the earth for a garden, hoeing and tilling. She planted half runners, potatoes, nasturtiums, corn, and beans. She wrote some letters to distant family. She went to Sunday school and church and played a game of Scrabble with a friend. She cleaned around the flowerbed and swept the walk. She worked in her garden again on Saturday and called her son Nelson on Sunday to say she wasn't feeling well, that something was wrong—this from a woman who had been sick just once in her life. Nelson dispatched an ambulance and raced to the hospital, flanked by a sympathetic highway patrolman, and found his mother in a coma.

The next morning, June 4, 1973, Nelson's wife and sister were sitting beside Emma's bed when she opened her eyes, closed them again, then hummed a few bars of "The Battle Hymn of the Republic"—*Mine eyes have seen the glory of the coming of the Lord . . .*

The obituaries said she "gained national and world fame" for her hikes. One quoted her daughter Rowena, who told of how Emma had learned of the trail from a magazine article. "She said, 'If those men can do it, I can do it.'"

The Ohio Senate passed a resolution in her memory, noting her accomplishments, that she was a founder of the Buckeye Trail, and that she had "inspired many, particularly young people, toward an interest in and an appreciation for the outdoors and in the relationship between man and his natural environment."

They lowered Emma Rowena Gatewood into the ground on a pretty hillside in the Ohio Valley Memorial Gardens in Gallia County. Her marker says simply:

EMMA R. GATEWOOD

GRANDMA

JUNE 7, 2012

Lucy Gatewood Seeds sits alone inside the lodge of a mountain resort in Boiling Springs, Pennsylvania, waiting for her family to dress for dinner. She stares out the large glass windows at the tall trees surrounding the lodge, listening for birds. She's not as good at identifying their songs as she once was, but if she listens long enough, the names come back.

She wears her eighty-four years well. Her gray hair is cut short and her bangs curl toward her forehead. The top button is buttoned on her flowered blouse.

Most of her family is here. Two sons and a daughter, and three grandchildren. Her sister, Louise, will arrive soon.

Lucy spots a man walking down the pavement toward the lodge. He is bearded and wearing a large backpack, covered by a rain tarp. The man is soaking wet when he steps inside. He doesn't remove his pack, but stands near the door and shakes water from his hands.

Lucy waves and the man smiles back.

"Did you come from the trail?" she asks.

"Yes, ma'am," the man says. "Just now."

"I'm Lucy Gatewood Seeds," Lucy says as the man approaches. "Grandma Gatewood was my mother."

"You're kidding!" the man says, reaching out his hand. "I read about your mama and I just couldn't believe it. It just really moved me."

Lucy smiles.

"She did it three times, right?" the man asks.

"Two thru-hikes and once in sections," Lucy replies. "And she went from Mount Oglethorpe, not Springer Mountain, where the trail starts today. So it was a little longer."

"She's one of the big reasons I'm here," he says. "I'm Stats."

"Hi, Stats," she says. "I'm Lucy."

She hugs the wet man like it doesn't matter.

"Grandma Gatewood," he says. "That's a name I haven't forgotten."

Stats's real name is Chris Odom and he's a physicist and former rocket scientist who now teaches physics at a Quaker boarding school. This is his eighty-seventh day on the trail and he decided to stay in the lodge, near the halfway point, because he's meeting his family soon. He first heard of the trail twenty-two years ago, in college, when he saw a map on the wall of his girlfriend's father's home. He asked about it, and the father sent him home with a two-volume set of books about the A.T. One of the stories was about Grandma Gatewood.

"Mrs. Emma Gatewood, better known along the trail as Grandma Gatewood, is probably the best-known of all the hikers who have completed the 2,000 miles of the Appalachian Trail," the story read. "Almost every through hiker has his favorite story about Grandma, which he has heard along the trail. She is the kind of personality about whom legends grow."

He wants a photo with Lucy. They stand near the fireplace.

"Now, what did you think?" he asks Lucy. "You were a grown woman when she set out. Were you worried?"

"No, no, no," Lucy says. "My mother was amazing."

"She started the spark for me twenty-two years ago," Stats says. "Your mom's story just captivated me."

This is the amazing reality of Grandma Gatewood's legacy. Somehow her story became a motivating tale for those who came in contact with it, man or woman, regardless of generation. Her hikes brought attention to the trail like none before. That's true as well for Ken "Buckeye" Bordwell, wearing a long white beard and hiking boots, who introduces himself to Lucy. He first heard of the A.T. when his father read stories about Emma aloud at their home in Cincinnati. His father followed her progress in the newspapers, tuned in to the old woman walking. In junior high school, Ken started to fantasize about setting out himself.

"That was one of the things that put it in my mind and made me a sitting duck for the 'Appalachian Trail Disease,'" he said. "There are certain ones among us who hear about the A.T., and then it's all over."

He started chipping off sections of the trail in 1965 and completed his final section last summer. "She helped many people become aware of the trail," Bordwell says. "She may have been one of the greatest publicists the trail ever had. A single, elderly woman, walking the whole thing? You can't buy publicity like that."

Gene Espy, the second thru-hiker, is here, too. The old Boy Scout hadn't heard about Grandma Gatewood's hikes until the 1970s, but they impressed him. He had trail guides, to say nothing of his pup tent and solid backpacking gear. "I thought that was a pretty good trick that she was able to carry her pack on her shoulder like that," he said. "You need your hands for climbing and whatnot. I thought it was a pretty good trick."

The reach of her story is hard to measure in any scientific way. But in the twenty years since the Internet brought us connectivity, many hikers have taken to journaling online about their outdoor experiences, and a search of one of the popular hosting sites—TrailJournals.com—turns up more "Grandma Gatewood" entries than you'd ever care to read. Some are calls to press forward—"Remember Grandma Gatewood!" and that kind of thing. Others speak to a deeper influence.

"Back when I was just a kid, my family belonged to and was active in a group called the National Campers & Hikers Association. I met 'Grandma' Gatewood, when she was the guest of honor at the first NCHA convention that I attended with my parents and sister at Lake of the Ozarks State Park in Missouri," wrote a hiker called Granny Franny. "She led us kids on hikes around trails in the state park, and I really enjoyed this feisty old lady who hiked. 'When I grow up, I'm going to do that,' I told myself."

"Over the years the story of Grandma Gatewood has remained in my mind and served as inspiration when I thought about all the reasons why I might not be able to do this hike," wrote a woman called Rockie.

"On the way up to the top of Mt. Guyot, I encountered the spirit of Grandma Gatewood," wrote Gatorgump. "She approached me as I was gasping for breath and feeling faint. I recognized her immediately from old photographs."

Among those who study the trail, those who know its history inside and out, her legacy is indelible. "She drew a lot of attention to the Appalachian Trail," said Larry Luxenberg, author of *Walking the Appalachian Trail*. "Her hikes inspired a lot of people. No matter how bad your hike is, how difficult the trail is, you could always point to Grandma Gatewood and say, 'Well, she did it.' "

Beyond the attention, and beyond her well-documented criticism that prompted better maintenance and upkeep, her hikes crumbled the psychological barrier that existed between the American public and this long path through the wilderness. She introduced people to the A.T., and at the same time she made the thru-hike achievable. It didn't take fancy equipment, guidebooks, training, or youthfulness. It took putting one foot in front of the other—five million times.

"She boasted that she was the only one of the thru-hikers of the Trail that really roughed it, and she was probably right," Ed Garvey said before he died. "She lacked most of the pieces of equipment that hikers consider absolutely essential, but she possessed that one ingredient, desire, in such full measure that she never really needed the other things."

Many A.T. scholars, Luxenberg included, point to Garvey as the man who turned on America to the thru-hike. It's true that his book, *Appalachian Hiker*, which offered practical advice, was popular; when he died in 1999, it was in its third edition. The book—and Garvey's hike—also received a fair amount of attention from the popular press. Part of the reason so many point to Garvey's thru-hike in 1970 and his subsequent book as an A.T. turning-point is because the number of thru-hikers began to rise significantly around the same time. From 1936 to 1969, only fifty-nine completions were recorded. From 1970 to 1979, 760 completions were recorded—a huge spike. That doubled in the 1980s, then doubled again in the 1990s. Nearly six thousand people hiked the entire length of the A.T. between 2000 and 2009. And it all seemed to start with Garvey's book.

But let's split hairs for a moment. In 1964, the year Emma Gatewood completed the entirety of the trail for the third time, four others finished as well. The following three years saw just eight completions. Then, in 1968, six hikers finished. In 1969, ten finished. Ten more completed the trail in 1970, the year of Garvey's hike. The surprise comes in 1971, when that number doubles—twenty-one people completed two-thousand-mile hikes that year, the most ever and more than double the number of two-thousand-milers from the year before. Here's the thing: it wasn't until December 1, 1971, after those twenty-one hikes were finished, that *Appalachian Hiker* was released. So, with all due respect to the late Mr. Garvey, the spike started before his book.

"She opened the door of knowledge of the trail to the general public," said Robert Croyle, membership secretary for the Appalachian Trail Museum and an accomplished outdoorsman. "Her hike brought attention to the trail that was sorely needed. Interest in the trail that she created caused interest in maintaining the trail, and that's carried on through today."

"She has become a folk icon and a symbol of the A.T. being for any American," said Laurie Potteiger, information services manager for the Appalachian Trail Conservancy. "She is in a class by herself. Earl Shaffer has his own legacy, but in terms of a folk hero, she has a special place in A.T. history. Her story is immediately fascinating."

Lucy Gatewood Seeds is here in Boiling Springs with her family because Grandma Gatewood is being inducted into the Appalachian Trail Hall of Fame, and, in a way, Lucy is the keeper of the flame. She's the youngest of Emma's four surviving children, who have all lived good, long lives. Lucy has kept her mother's correspondence, journals, and photographs. She makes copies of newspaper clippings and journal entries and puts together scrapbooks to share with those who are interested. She has lent to museums her inherited memora-bilia—old shoes, Band-Aid tins, and denim sacks. And she protects her mother's legacy. When Lucy learned that the author Bill Bryson had mentioned her mother in his best-selling book about the A.T., she found the passage, then found it unflattering.

"Probably the most famous, certainly the most written about, of all thru-hikers was Emma 'Grandma' Gatewood," Bryson wrote, "who successfully hiked the trail twice in her late sixties despite being eccentric, poorly equipped, and a danger to herself. (She was forever getting lost.)"

Lucy fired off a letter to the witty writer, who hiked only 39.5 percent of the A.T. himself.

"Eccentric, perhaps, but kindly, please. Lost, never, just mis-directed," she wrote. "I hope you have the satisfaction of completing the trail some day."

These are Lucy's moments. She was disheartened to learn that her mother wasn't in the inaugural Hall of Fame class, which included Myron Avery, Gene Espy, Ed Garvey, Benton MacKaye, Arthur Perkins, and Earl Shaffer. She let it be known. When the second class was announced, she was pleased.

"When I'm dead and gone," Emma told Lucy and Louise once, in a tone that was certain and not at all arrogant, "they're going to erect monuments to me."

She was right. In the Hall of Fame down the road, her wooden bust is on a mantle and a display case tells her story. She came to pioneer three separate groups of A.T. hikers: seniors, women, and "ultra-light," a style of minimalist hiking, carrying as little gear as possible, which has recently come into vogue. She was even the inspiration for a lightweight rain cape that doubles as a shelter—the Gatewood Cape.

She also remains in elite company. Nearly four decades after her third A.T. jaunt, just eight women and fifty-five men have completed three two-thousand-mile hikes, according to Appalachian Trail Conservancy records.

"She was so proud of all she had done, and she had gotten so much public attention from it," said Louise. "She figured that it was going to be noteworthy and people were going to remember her."

When it's time for the ceremony, Lucy is ready. She has delivered versions of the same speech before, but this night is special. The hall at the Allenberry Resort Inn is packed with hikers, politicians, and philanthropists, those with interest in preserving the A.T. for the next generation. They speak of the trail's importance and its tentative future, how development threatens and protecting the wilderness is in everyone's interest. When they began speaking of the pioneers, Larry Luxenberg talks about Emma.

"Most women would have been content to live out their lives in comfort," he says.

"Many call her the first thru-hiker celebrity," he says.

"She was a hiker for the ages," he says.

Lucy is called to the podium. The crowd sits silently.

"People call her Grandma Gatewood," Lucy says, "but I call her mamma."

— — — — —

They still ask.

Wherever Lucy goes, whenever Grandma Gatewood comes up in conversation, people want to know why she did what she did. No surprise there. The question in general has prompted at least one scholarly study, in 2007, called *Why Individuals Hike the Appalachian Trail: A Qualitative Approach to Benefits*. The researchers found that common reasons were the standard fare: being outdoors, hiking, the fun and enjoyment of life, warm relationships, physical challenge, camaraderie, solitude, and survival.

It's easy enough, I guess, to take Emma's various responses at face value. Maybe she never thought too long or hard about why she wanted to test herself against nature. Maybe the first time was a lark, as she said, or some primal need to see what was over the next hill, then the next. That might explain the first trip, but then she learned how difficult it was, how painful, how the rosy *National Geographic* article had been wrong.

And she did it again. And again. That's where my understanding begins to fall short. We could, of course, leave it at her being eccentric, as Bill Bryson wrote, but that's far too easy an explanation. She did, after all, keep good company on the trail, making friends who were very glad to see her on her return, and not in some sideshow kind of way. She was well read, well spoken, and white-gloves proper. It's true that she could twitch her gentility slightly to let you know you had done or said something of which she didn't approve. But to suggest she was eccentric is to suggest it would be strange for her to walk. We know that she couldn't drive, and that it wasn't out of the ordinary for her to walk five or ten miles to visit a friend in the course of her daily life. The long hikes were simply an extension of that, a means of getting from point A to point B. Eccentric? No.

Lucy believes that her mother wanted to be the first woman to thru-hike the trail, and that's worth thinking about. A minor problem with that theory arises when you consider that the story that introduced her to the trail was written in 1949, five years before she set out the first time, in '54. There's no indication that Emma saw or read anything about the trail in that span, so how would she have known whether another woman had completed the hike? Maybe Lucy is right in a general sense—but if being the first of her gender was the primary motivating factor, wouldn't she have made certain that no other woman had gone before her?

I believe Emma Gatewood was honest. I also believe there's an equal chance that her stock answers were covers. They were honest—and also incomplete—responses to a question she couldn't bring herself to fully answer, not when she was a "widow." Not when she had a secret. Not when she had tasted her own blood, felt her ribs crack, and seen the inside of a jail cell. To suggest she was trying to be the first woman means believing that she was walking toward

something. I'm not sure that's wholly true. I'm not sure she was walking toward something so much as walking away.

There's one response among the dozens that I've come to think best answers the question, a declarative sentence in the public record that is equal parts truth and defiance. It's a statement that betrays a secret at the same time. There's something both bold and hidden in the response. Something beautiful and independent, mysterious and brave. There is escape between the words. Escape from abuse and oppression. Escape from age and obligation. It ends with a period that might as well be a question mark, four words that launch a thousand ships, and it's an answer that frustrates and satisfies.

"Because," she told a reporter, "I wanted to."

EPILOGUE

Before dawn on the third Saturday of January 2013, I drove Louise Gatewood LaMott from her condominium north of Columbus, Ohio, to Hocking Hills State Park, a few hours southeast. When we arrived, the lots surrounding the park were filling and families began piling out of cars and forming lines beside three or four school buses, which, when filled, ferried them down the hill to the trailhead.

The morning was downright cold, near freezing, and the hikers came prepared. They were bundled head to toe in the best gear—Patagonia, Columbia, the North Face, Eagle Creek, Camelbak. Keys dangled from carabiners and ski poles hung from wrists. They stuffed chemical hand-warmers into their pockets. I watched a middle-aged man and woman sit and strap spiked contraptions on the bottoms of their shoes, like snow chains for hiking boots.

Louise, God love her, was wearing a gray jacket, slacks, and low-top Nike sneakers. "I don't think I'll need my gloves," she said as we climbed out of the rental. She'll be eighty-seven in two months and as much as I wanted to, I wasn't going to second-guess her. ("My daughters treat me like a child," she had told me a few times before, more of a statement to me than an indictment of them.)

When I flew into Columbus, it honestly hadn't occurred to me that she might want to accompany me to Hocking Hills. I had simply called to say hello, and see if I might swing by to visit before heading down to the forty-eighth-annual winter hike. But she insisted, and here she stood in the cold, clutching her mother's skinny stick. Forty years after Grandma Gatewood's last winter hike, her daughter was not going to miss it.

The other thing I hadn't expected was the crowd. I'm a fan of state parks, and I visit them often. I've seen full campsites at beautiful Big Bend down in southwest Texas and packed freshwater springs on hot Florida afternoons, but I've never in my life seen this many people occupy one park at the same time. The scene—minus the camouflage coveralls and checkerboard hunting caps—looked like a rock concert. Thousands had come—young and old, skinny and obese. Cars were packed on the grass in all directions. Walking down a single row, I saw license plates from West Virginia, Illinois, Michigan, Kentucky, and, strangely, New Mexico. I half-expected to find a carnival stand selling funnel cakes.

We stood in the cold for thirty minutes before we could get on one of the buses. When we got to the trailhead, *there was a line.* I can't emphasize this enough. To get onto the trail near Old Man's Cave, there was a queue like you'd find at the most popular roller coaster at an amusement park. People were waiting on the buses, then waiting at the trailhead one-hundred-deep . . . *to take a walk.* To see nature. To descend from level ground down to Old Man's Cave, to a geographically secretive underground world with these huge *Jurassic Park*–like trees, these gorgeous waterfalls and blackhand sandstone recesses made slowly, particle by particle, over thousands of years.

That morning, I guessed out loud that there were three thousand others walking with us. I'd learn later that 4,305 people showed up to hike six miles. Think about that for a minute.

Many of them wore patches that said Grandma Gatewood Hike. A big boulder was planted at the trailhead, where the clogged line waited for a bottleneck to clear. A large metal plaque affixed to the rock said:

GRANDMA GATEWOOD MEMORIAL TRAIL
THIS SIX-MILE TRAIL IS DEDICATED TO THE MEMORY OF
GRANDMA GATEWOOD, A VIBRANT WOMAN, SEASONED HIKER,
AND LONG-TIME HOCKING HILLS ENTHUSIAST. THE PATH BEGINS HERE,
VISITS CEDAR FALLS, AND TERMINATES AT ASH CAVE.
JANUARY 17, 1981

I thought of what Louise had told me about her mother. "When I'm dead and gone," Emma said, "they're going to erect monuments to me." She knew. The Grandma Gatewood Trail has come to be part of the cross-state, twelve-hundred-mile Buckeye Trail, part of the forty-six hundred-mile federal North Country Trail that runs from New York to North Dakota, and part of the American Discovery Trail that covers sixty-eight-hundred miles from Delaware to California.

We slowly and carefully snaked into the gorge, down a series of slopes and worn steps set in stone as trail volunteers sprinkled rock salt at our feet to melt the snow and ice. Even in a crowd, this felt like sacred ground. There was no question why Emma liked this place so much, why she thought it was the most interesting geographical feature she'd seen. Old Man's Cave is a recess in the side of a cliff, about seventy-five feet above the rushing stream. And it's big—250 feet long and about 50 feet high.

"You might have to put me on your back," Louise said.

I was ready to, but she braved the stone steps and icy bridges like a younger woman. I imagined her mother doing the same thing on her final hike, with men reaching out to steady her, to carry her over the rough patches.

Thinking of that scene makes me whimper. We had spoken with a man in line earlier who had participated in this same hike for more

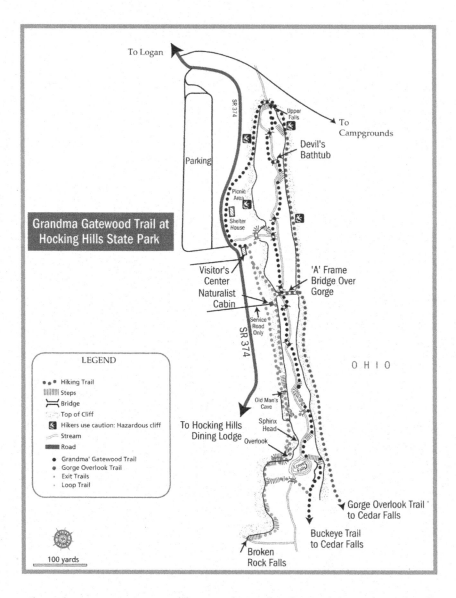

To Logan

SR 374

Parking

Upper
Falls

To
Campgrounds

Devil's
Bathtub

Picnic
Area

Shelter
House

Grandma Gatewood Trail at
Hocking Hills State Park

Visitor's
Center
Naturalist
Cabin

'A' Frame
Bridge Over
Gorge

Service
Road
Only

SR 374

O H I O

LEGEND

- Hiking Trail
- Steps
- Bridge
- Top of Cliff
- Hikers use caution: Hazardous cliff
- Stream
- Road

- Grandma' Gatewood Trail
- Gorge Overlook Trail
- Exit Trails
- Loop Trail

Old Man's
Cave

To Hocking Hills
Dining Lodge

Sphinx
Head

Overlook

Lower
Falls

Gorge Overlook Trail
to Cedar Falls

Buckeye Trail
to Cedar Falls

100 yards

Broken
Rock Falls

than thirty years. He couldn't explain what keeps him coming back, but I think I know. I think I know why Louise insisted on coming, and I think I know why I booked a plane ticket on a moment's notice, just twenty-four hours before. I think I know why all these people line up by that big plaque on the boulder every year and funnel—baby step–by–baby step—onto the Grandma Gatewood Trail. To be here is to participate in an experience, *her* experience. To walk this path that she loved is to embrace her memory, to come as close to her as possible. To see what she saw and step where she stepped and feel some thin connection to a farm woman who decided one day to take a walk, and then kept going, getting faster until the end. I could be imagining all this, but I lost myself a little. In her footsteps, I forgot my troubles. Maybe the fountain of youth wasn't a fountain at all.

Louise made it over her mother's trail just fine. I held her arm through the icy patches, but she didn't need it. I drove her back to Columbus, and we agreed to do it again next year.

ACKNOWLEDGMENTS

I may not have known about Grandma Gatewood if it weren't for my mother, Donna Burruss, handing down the stories she inherited. I remember them fondly, dreamy tales of adventure and mystery. Conversations with her siblings, especially Lou Terry, helped immensely.

Thanks to Emma's surviving children, Louise, Rowena, Nelson, and especially Lucy, who all opened their homes and sacrificed many hours of their time to help me understand their mother as they knew her. They also kindly granted me access to her correspondence, photographs, and journals without asking anything in return. I'm in their debt.

Thanks to Bill Duryea and Kelley Benham for their advice and feedback, and to Michael Kruse, who was always willing to listen. My other generous colleagues at the *Tampa Bay Times* were understanding when I blew deadlines or disappeared because of book work, and they offered tons of unsolicited encouragement and advice. They are Neil Brown, Mike Wilson, Leonora LaPeter Anton, Lane DeGregory, Jeff Klinkenberg, Laura Reiley, Janet Keeler, Eric Deggans, Craig Pittman, and Mary Jane Park. John Capouya, Tom French, Neil Swidey, Michael Brick, Hank Stuever, Chris Jones, Earl Swift, and Matthew Algeo helped me understand what makes a good book, and how to sell it. Speaking of selling it, my agent Jane Dystel held my hand through the entire daunting process.

There's no finer linear community in America than the folks who know, love, and preserve the Appalachian Trail. I can't possibly thank all the people who opened their homes to me, gave me rides, or helped me find my way along the trail, but I'd like to thank Laurie Potteiger, Larry Luxenberg, Paul Sannicandro, Robert Croyle, Betsy Bainbridge, Paul Renaud, Gene Espy, Peter Thomson, and Bjorn Kruse. Thanks, too, to a handful of librarians in small towns and cities along the trail who helped track down old stories about Emma's journey.

Finally, this book would not be possible without my wife, Jennifer, who kept me organized and took care of our family while I chased Emma Gatewood's ghost across the country. She even climbed Mount Katahdin on an injured ankle to see the journey complete. My children, Asher, Morissey, and Bey, deserve credit as well for asking a thousand times: "Are you done with the book yet, Daddy?"

Yes, I am.

BIBLIOGRAPHY

Agee, James, and Walker Evans. *Let Us Now Praise Famous Men.* Boston: Houghton Mifflin Co., 1939.

Amato, Joseph A. *On Foot: A History of Walking.* New York: New York University Press, 2004.

Bryson, Bill. *A Walk in the Woods.* New York: Broadway Books, 1998.

Espy, Gene. *The Trail of My Life.* Macon, GA: Indigo Publishing, 2008.

George, Jean Craighead. *The American Walk Book.* New York: E.P. Dutton, 1978.

Hare, James. *Hiking the Appalachian Trail, Volume One.* Emmaus, PA: Rodale Press, Inc., 1975.

Hare, James. *Hiking the Appalachian Trail, Volume Two.* Emmaus, PA: Rodale Press, Inc., 1975.

Luxenberg, Larry. *Walking the Appalachian Trail.* Mechanicsburg, PA: Stackpole Books, 1994.

Marshall, Ian. *Storyline: Exploring the Literature of the Appalachian Trail.* Charlottesville, VA: University of Virginia Press, 1998.

Matthews, Estivaun, Charles A. Murray, and Pauline Rife. *Gallia County One-Room Schools: The Cradle Years.* Ann Arbor, MI: Braun-Brumfield, Inc., 1993.

Morse, Joseph Laffan. *The Unicorn Book of 1953.* New York: Unicorn Books, Inc. 1954.

Morse, Joseph Laffan. *The Unicorn Book of 1954*. New York: Unicorn Books, Inc. 1955.

Morse, Joseph Laffan. *The Unicorn Book of 1955*. New York: Unicorn Books, Inc. 1956.

Nicholson, Geoff. *The Lost Art of Walking: The History, Science, Philosophy and Literature of Pedestrianism*. New York: Riverhead Books, 2008.

Seagrave, Kerry. *America on Foot: Walking and Pedestrianism in the 20th Century*. Jefferson, NC: McFarland and Company, Inc.

Shaffer, Earl V. *Walking with Spring: The First Solo Thru-Hike of the Legendary Appalachian Trail*. Harpers Ferry, WV: Appalachian Trail Conference, 1996.

Solnit, Rebecca. *Wanderlust: A History of Walking*. New York: Penguin Books, 2000.

Swift, Earl. *The Big Roads: The Untold Story of the Engineers, Visionaries, and Trailblazers Who Created the American Superhighways*. Boston: Houghton Mifflin Harcourt, 2011.

INDEX